A MILLION BUCKS BY 30

BALLANTINE BOOKS NEW YORK

A MILLION BUCKS BY 30

How to Overcome a Crap Job, Stingy Parents, and a Useless Degree to Become a Millionaire Before (or After) Turning Thirty

Alan Corey

A Ballantine Books Trade Paperback Original

Published in the United States by Ballantine Books, an imprint of
The Random House Publishing Group, a division of Random House, Inc.,
New York.

BALLANTINE and colophon are registered trademarks of
Random House, Inc.

Library of Congress Cataloging-in-Publication Data

Corey, Alan.
A million bucks by 30 : how to overcome a crap job, stingy parents,
and a useless degree to become a millionaire before (or after) turning
thirty / Alan Corey.
   p.   cm.
ISBN 978-0-345-49972-1
1. Finance, Personal.   2. Saving and investment.   3. Investments.
4. Businesspeople—United States—Biography.   I. Title.
II. Title: Million bucks by thirty.
HG179.C6825   2008
332.024'01—dc22   2007028326

www.ballantinebooks.com

Book design by Glen M. Edelstein

147028622

This amazingly awesome book is dedicated to my parents, Nancy and Larry. Mom, don't worry, there shouldn't be any embarrassing grammar mistakes. Dad, thanks for buying this before it hits the bargain bin.

Just to be clear, this amazingly awesome book is not dedicated to my sister, Jill.

Contents

Introduction

OKAY, here's me in a nutshell: Coming out of college, I was scared of the opposite sex, I hated where I lived, I had no viable skills, and the worst of it, I was flat broke. Maybe right now you are better off than I was, maybe worse, but I was in a place where I wanted a change. To change everything. I wanted something better. It wasn't peachy being a newly sprung college grad with a crappy day job, trying to get by in my suburban hometown living in my mom's basement among abandoned exercise equipment and slowly leaking beanbag chairs. It didn't take me long to figure out that wasn't the way I wanted to live—that is, on someone else's terms and schedule, with a limited social calendar, and, not to mention, under financial constraints. So, at the age of twenty-two, I happened upon an idea so crazy I thought it just might work: I would become a millionaire by the time I was thirty.

Of course, I wasn't the first person to set this goal, but I'm not sure how many people actually accomplish it, and my guess is that those who have probably went about it differently than I did.

You see, I'm just a plain ol' gravelly voiced dude with no special talents. I didn't become an investment banker or a high-powered lawyer, and my family's not loaded. When I decided to be a millionaire by thirty, I had just accepted a job in a new town, leaving behind a ridiculous comfort zone of familiar surroundings and friends. And, of course, my mom's weekly Chore Wheel. I left that all behind to make $40,000 a year as a technical-support guy in one of the most expensive cities in the world. I definitely didn't know what I was getting into, but I was excited about it.

I embarked on my new life with a freshly printed college diploma and $10,000 to my name. That's a lot of money for a twenty-two-year-old. But because I made some solid financial decisions before and during college, I was leaving school ahead of my friends, financially speaking. I went to a university that offered me a full scholarship, and I kept it all four years. (That doesn't mean I'm smart; it just means my college had loose standards.) It wasn't the school of my dreams, but I knew I could make it work. It took me a semester or two, but I eventually found a way to balance my studies and keg stands (both required someone shouting "Hurry! Before the girls/cops get here!").

Another chunk of that ten grand came from money I had been saving since sixth grade. My mother, in an effort to make me interested in personal finance, had promised to double any amount of money I deposited into my savings account. Looking back on it now, it made no sense for her to teach me the value of money by giving me free money. But I took her offer as lesson number one in personal finance: Refusing free money is stupid. My $20 weekly allowance for mowing the lawn quickly became a $40-a-week bank deposit. Same with the money I was earning from mowing my neighbors' lawns. And their neighbors' lawns. After a few months of crazy lawn-mowing binges, my mom reneged on her deal (teaching me another lesson about free money: It ain't forever). She thought I was taking advantage of her offer, but I'd like to think I was just being opportunistic (something I'll get into in more detail later in the book). Regardless of the lost matching contributions, I kept adding to my savings account throughout middle school and high school. My job dressing up as the Chuck E. Cheese's rat earned me a regular paycheck, as did occasional lifeguarding and coaching duties at the local YMCA. And even in high school, I kept mowing all those lawns. Twenty dollars for an hour's work is hard to pass up, especially to someone with a limited skill set like me.

Like most, I continued working in college. I still lifeguarded for a bit, waited tables, and bartended. I even earned a big payday by becoming an accidental entrepreneur. My roommate Jeff and I wanted to throw the biggest party possible in the field next to our house. We rented generators and Porta Pottis, hired bands, advertised on radio stations and in newspapers, and bought fifteen kegs for the party. It was a bit risky and definitely a lot of work, but we each invested a sizable portion of our savings to do it. At a minimum, we just wanted to recoup our expenses.

So we had to charge $5 a head. It paid off, though: We had generated so much buzz among all the students that more than six hundred people came! Jeff and I made over $2,000 in unforeseen profit. It was an amazing feeling seeing that much cash on our living room table. If it were sitting in a suitcase, I would have sworn we had done something illegal. Okay, full disclosure: Considering that I was twenty, I *was* doing something illegal. But it was a memorable and profitable night due to our foresight of securing party permits and observing noise ordinances. Memorable and profitable mainly because for once it didn't require yelling "Hurry, before the cops get here!"

Anyway, that was then, and this is now. With $10,000 in savings and a dream, I did become a millionaire by the time I was thirty. The point of this book is to let you know that you can too.

In the following chapters, I'll break down exactly *how* I made a million bucks, and the strategies and steps I took along the way. None of them involves selling kidneys from a Las Vegas bathtub, but, you know, what happens in Vegas stays in Vegas, *especially if it's your sold-off kidney.* But they do involve key financial decisions that I made: my journey from fledgling real-estate investor, to landlord, to seven-figure flipper, and the gory details about my life as (according to most of the people I've dated) one of the biggest cheapskates on the planet.

At the end of every chapter, I'll show you how I'm doing with a running tally of exactly how much cash I've got to my name, as well as a final "Alan Corey 101." Throughout the book you'll see boldfaced financial terms. Simply turn to the glossary for an explanation of what they mean.

Read the book any way you want. Read it from start to finish; read just the lessons, tips, and box scores; or, if you don't really like me yet, read it from back to front and watch me go from a millionaire to being broke.

My hope is that you'll see that there is no magic secret to being a millionaire, but, instead, that with focus, dedication, creativity, and sacrifice, you can earn a big payday just like me. Not everything I did will apply to your circumstances or appeal to your lifestyle. (Eating ramen every day for three months may be one of them.) But I'm confident that many of my strategies will work, or, at the very least, will serve as the inspiration for you to come up with your own creative financial solutions. Hopefully, legal, conscience-friendly solutions (or at least kidney-friendly ones). Regardless, the basic principles that got me rich are universal, and the best news is that putting them into action is absolutely free.

In short: If I can do it, so can you. Good luck on your path to creating your very own million, and, most of all, have fun! I sure did.

Alan Corey

PART I

Scrounging, Scheming, and Saving

Chapter 1
Naïve in New York

THIS was me:

Wait, I just graduated from college? No more classes???
That was my last test? Does this mean I can't do what other col-
lege kids are doing now? I want to be with them, eating filth,
drinking filth, and living in filth—that's my life. I can't stop
doing that. Every day, 99-cent hot dogs, 99-cent beers, and
99-cent toilet paper. The 99-cent store rules! I can't leave. Oh
man, what about the girls? So many girls! Some of them are actu-
ally attracted to me, even with my complete disregard of normal
bathing and laundry habits. You know how a shirt is either clean
or "college clean"? That's me every day: college clean. Haven't
shaved since Easter, either. I am living the perfect life. I am within
a short walk of every single friend of mine, not to mention every
single bar, and on top of all that, I am financing this utopian
lifestyle on my meager income from coaching basketball at the Y. I
don't want to get a real job. There are worse lives for sure, but none
that I can think of that are better. Damn, I should have stretched
this out for five years like everyone else. What the hell am I going

to do now? I can't be that guy who sticks around college for no reason. I mean, I can be, but I don't want to be. I hate that guy. Barb the guidance counselor says to go get a real job. Yeah, thanks, Barb. My parents must have called her and fed her that line. A real job?? Doing what? It's not like she does anything great.

Honestly, I didn't know what my major was until my second to last semester of college. I finally settled on management of information systems. What the Fran Tarkenton is an "information system"? And why does it need managing? That's what I'm majoring in??? Barb told me that if I changed my major, I wouldn't be able to graduate in four years. So I'm stuck with it. Luckily, my older friend Clay majored in MIS too, and he coached me through my last two semesters in college. He explained that my major was about computers—databases, specifically—and that I'd make big money once I was done with school. I decided I could live with that. Like most business students, the prospect of a huge salary could motivate me through anything.

I finally graduated two semesters later and was thrown headfirst into full-fledged adulthood. Adulthood is bizarre! All of a sudden I was above couch surfing, started caring about the weather forecast, and was drinking microbrews. What the Fran Drescher was happening to me? I was turning into my dad! Or even *his* dad.

But that's what real jobs do to you. You start earning something above minimum wage for once, and you start thinking like an adult. I had been so happy being a broke guy with an open schedule. Hell, everyone was broke and had an open schedule. Now that I had a job, I couldn't plan anything with anyone. I had entered this whole new world of regular working hours and paychecks. It took considerable self-discipline and self-control for me to handle this awkward transition. Once again, my buddy Clay helped me through it. It took many beers (microbrewed beer), but I got over it.

My first *real* job after college was in Atlanta, building computers for a family friend. It didn't pay a whole lot, but it had perks. No dress code, you say? Then college clean it is! Although I wasn't making big bucks, the job allowed me to buy time to figure out what I really wanted to do with my life. Believe me, living in my mom's basement (which was the current state of affairs) was not what I wanted to do with the rest of my life.

On my drive to work every day, I would strategize about where my life should go. Rock star? Fireman? Evil genius? I considered everything. My one obstacle was that I didn't have anything to fall back on except a diploma in something I didn't care about. I was lost. I felt that to be truly happy, I had to leave my comfort zone and my hometown behind. I always liked being a little uncomfortable; it meant that I was learning something. I couldn't figure out if I wanted to move to New York, Australia, or somewhere in Europe. I knew Los Angeles had hot women, so it was always at the top of my list. I figured there had to be some attractive woman on the beach who needed her information system managed. If only she could find my résumé!

For my first five months at work, I saved as much

money as I could out of each paycheck. In between building computers, I sent out résumés. I sent them to every computer-based job opening in New York, Los Angeles, and overseas. I wanted a change, a location change, but it wasn't coming easy. Of the more than seven hundred fifty résumés sent, I got two viable replies.

The first response was from Dublin, Ireland, and they wanted to know if I knew some programming language that I had never heard of before. A response of "willing to learn" did not get me the job. But I didn't stop searching. Looking back now, I'm pretty sure it was my lack of a professional résumé that garnered me only two decent replies. Using the word *proficient* on a résumé has a point of diminishing returns after its tenth appearance.

My e-mail address at the time was the first one I had out of school. That meant I got to pick it out myself! I thought that Yahoo! and AOL were way too conventional for a dynamic person like me, so I wanted an address that would help me stand out; something that would help me make big money in a big city! I also wanted something to help me meet some ladies. (That's my motivation with most things in life; it's a wonder I'm not a production assistant on *The View.*) I also wanted something free. (Okay, *that's* really my motivation in life.) So after some trolling around the ol' Net, I registered something free, fun, and what I thought might impress the chicks: BigAl@models.com. I honestly thought my MIS degree *and* a "modeling related" e-mail address were key requirements to making it big. Yes, of course, the plan backfired.

But not just because it was utterly lame. Another problem became apparent when I realized that everyone was reading my e-mail name (written "bigal") as "BiGal" rather than "BigAl." This was not exactly how I was trying to market myself to the world. I did get a whole lot of dudes contacting me, though. Dudes with plenty of offers, but not of the employment variety.

Twenty-one weeks into my get-out-of-my-mom's-basement campaign came my second reply, from a start-up company in New York that apparently read BigAl the way it was intended. A phone interview went well. An in-person interview went even better. And the next thing I knew, I was getting offered a job in NYC! I realized that a location change would make me happy, and that it was what my life needed. On top of that, I was relieved (and a bit proud) that I hadn't stopped sending out résumés until I achieved my goal. The real world would treat me okay as long as I followed my instincts and dreams—and didn't falsely represent myself as a female bisexual model.

This new job didn't have a high salary for Manhattan, and it wasn't a job in managing information systems, exactly. I was in charge of a 1-800 hotline and answering questions about the company's software. I figured I could do that short term, maybe get a real business e-mail address out of it, my first business card, and then pursue my life's ambitions. That is, once I figured out what those ambitions were. I knew I'd eventually find my path to earning the big bucks after my move to the big city, and that it wouldn't be from this job. But I felt that because I'd successfully

Extreme Cheapskate Strategy

Don't pay for Internet access. With more and more free Wi-Fi in public parks and on university campuses, you can pretty much log on from anywhere. You could even hijack your next-door neighbor's connection if necessary. If wireless isn't your thing, you can log on for free at most libraries or go to NetZero for free Internet access. Yes, it's dial-up, and you have a lot of ads, but free is free, and you can still check your e-mail, which is all you really use it for anyway.

changed my situation to be in New York, I couldn't be far off.

That January I moved into an apartment in Manhattan. It was during a snowstorm, and I unloaded my stuff with the help of my new roommate, a work-friend of a friend of a friend. My share of the rent was surprisingly cheap for New York City—$400 a month—but that was my payoff for obsessively hunting for an apartment. After scouring multiple real-estate sites, roommate sites, and firing off mass e-mails to everyone I thought might have a lead, I found a place so cheap, it seemed to wow everyone. And that $400 even included utilities! I didn't care what it looked like. I had agreed to it from my basement in Atlanta, sight unseen. I knew I would be happy just being in New York.

Upon arrival, I unloaded my stuff and finally got a tour

of the place. The apartment wasn't too bad. The wallpaper in the living room was yellowing, my room was painted pink, but, thankfully, the place had working faucets. Good enough for me! Anything was better than living back home and under my mother's rules. I was really happy (and proud once again) that I had upgraded my lifestyle in such a short amount of time. I was making it, sort of.

A month later two friends from home moved to New York and got an apartment within a short subway ride of me. Just twenty blocks from me, they were paying triple in rent for a smaller place. I encouraged them to keep looking for better deals, but they took the first place they could find. It seemed crazy to spend that much on rent. I knew their incomes were going to be even less than mine, but being fresh out of college, they wanted to "live it up" a bit. I wanted to make the point to them that "living it up" did not usually mean paying a fortune for a bad apartment, but then again, my steady diet of plain pizza and ramen eliminated me in their eyes as an expert on living it up.

While they spent their weekends shopping and decorating their apartment, I took my weekends to explore my neighborhood. I quickly learned that Spanish was the only language spoken within a ten-block radius. I had taken Spanish in high school, so I figured it would come back to me eventually. However, all I could recall was *"Yo bebo de vez en cuando la leche con mi abuela."* A phrase that is not helpful in any situation, really. No one, Spanish speaking or not, wants to hear that "I occasionally drink milk with my grandmother." Regardless of the communication failure I had with my neighbors, I was in heaven. I couldn't believe I accidentally ended up living in the coolest place in the world. Imagine being in one of the cultural pavilions of Epcot, but sans tourists in fluorescent ball caps, and you'll have an idea of what life was like for me. It was a dream come true. This was 180 degrees from the Atlanta suburbs, and it was amazing. My friends also loved their place in the more upscale part of the city, and I admit it did look nice. But it seemed to be a waste of money. My neighborhood had culture, flair, and character. I didn't see that where they lived. Their block seemed more manufactured and main-stream, or, basically, un–New York like.

I was happy to furnish my place with discarded furniture that I found on the sidewalk. It felt like my stuff had a story to tell, or an interesting life, and I was just putting it in my home to retire. New things didn't excite me, especially if I had to pay for them. I was already feeling the financial crunch of New York, and I had to save money every chance I could get.

A few months flew by. I got acquainted with the city and started to feel at home in my surroundings. I smiled at all my neighbors in the elevators and on the sidewalks. The one neighbor who did speak English always thought that I was my roommate; he would continue conversations with me that he'd had with *him,* and I chose to just feign under-standing him. I mean, we didn't look anything alike, but we were the only white guys around, so I didn't mind the slipup. But what I couldn't understand is why no one would visit me.

I had made some new friends in my short time in New York and told people where I lived, but no one would come by despite numerous invites. I wanted to show them the awesome restaurant on the corner where no one spoke English, and how big my place was for the little rent I paid, and the cool view of Yankee Stadium from my bedroom window. Basically, I wanted to show off. And then one day, five months into my New York residency, one of my friends in the nice apartment finally told me why they wouldn't come visit me. We were on the phone, and she huffed, "Alan, you want to know why we're not coming to your place? Because you live in the projects!"

The projects?!?! You know the projects you see in the rap videos? That was me. I was there. I was living in those projects. My roommate assumed I knew this the whole time and never mentioned it to me. I was a resident of the projects in Spanish Harlem in New York City for five months. Jesus H. Lopez! And the best thing was that no one in the neighborhood had ever given me any beef. Either I was innocently hardcore, or the projects just weren't that scary to me. I mean, I heard gunshots almost every other week, but I thought that was what living in New York was like, not what living in the projects was like. After checking to make sure that my underwear wasn't soiled, I patted my naïve self on the back. I thought it was pretty freaking cool. I let the news settle in—and then looked around, grinned real big, and couldn't wait to embrace more of these so-called projects. As far as I was concerned, this project was a success.

I had already found the 99-cent store there, but then I found a real cheap grocery store too. And that's all I needed. I was actually able to continue my college lifestyle a bit. My new job had my favorite perk. That's right, I was still *college clean* in New York. Plus, the projects made it hard to spend big since all the businesses there had a bargain angle to them. I was, in a way, forced to be thrifty. My friends back home were buying their first cars and new work wardrobes, and incurring other miscellaneous expenses, while I was content not being image conscious or spending money to match a new lifestyle. And it seemed to be what most people around me were doing too. I was hanging on to that college life, financially speaking, even with an honest-to-god salary. I loved my situation so much, I lived in the projects for another seven months. This wasn't just an apartment to me, it was my home.

As my friends made it pretty clear to me, living in the projects isn't for everyone. Obviously, no break in rent is worth not feeling comfortable in your neighborhood. That said, that doesn't mean you have to live in a super-fancy condo to feel safe. Living with a couple of roommates is a great way to be able to afford an apartment in a "nicer" neighborhood; you maybe sacrifice some privacy, but you often get more space for your money and a larger selection of places where you can afford to live. (Three bedrooms generally do not cost three times as much as one bedroom.) If you use public transportation, don't live in a place that's a desolate street or a long walk away from the train or bus. And if you feel uncomfortable going home late at night, by all means, take a cab and just budget for occasions like these.

I've found that the key to staying safe—both in and out of the projects—is being smart, confident, and alert. Don't walk with your head down and with headphones on in an unknown part of town. If you look like a victim, you are more likely to be targeted as a victim. However, things happen for no reason at all, so it's best to be alert and safe. Maybe living in the projects to save money isn't for you, but instead consider living in the uncool part of town. Or one with a farther drive. Or one known to have a lot of senior citizens (always bargain friendly).

Anyway, it's all about sacrifices for the greater good. This was my first lesson in New York finance: The more you give up, the more you gain. Choose wisely. It's far better to start out in the projects than it is to end up there.

ALAN COREY 101

Follow what makes you happy. If you have that feeling that you belong somewhere else, doing something else, being with someone else, you should follow that instinct. It is best to live life on your own terms. If it doesn't help you become a millionaire, it will at least make you a happier person. You are the catalyst for that change, and it's rarely easy to do. Major changes, like graduating from school, getting your first job, or moving to a new city, require being able to adapt easily. If you don't like it, make another

Alan's Strategies for Apartment Hunting

1. Inform everyone that you are looking for a place. That great deal might come from a friend of a coworker's pet-sitter's therapist.

2. Look a few months in advance. If you are looking for a great deal in a week, it's not going to happen. It's even less likely to happen when you are looking for a place within twenty-four hours.

3. Be willing to make sacrifices. The longer the commute, the more unsavory the neighborhood, or the lack of close restaurants usually means it'll have a much cheaper rent. You don't need to have the coolest place in the world right out of college. Postpone it until you have a million dollars.

4. Bargain with the landlord. Many landlords are willing to trade $50 a month for you to take care of all the extra stuff around the property (putting out trash, sweeping, mowing the yard, letting in repairmen, and so on). It doesn't hurt to request a two-year lease instead of a one-year lease in exchange for lower rent. The allure of a long-term and reliable tenant is worth it to most landlords. It should go without saying, but generally any nonshithead vibe you give your landlord is for the best. So always try to be nice!

5. Be willing to live with roommates. It could improve your people skills in a "how am I not going to kill him" sort of way and also could save you a bundle in cash.

6. Rent a furnished apartment, or just don't buy new things for your rented apartment. That beautiful new $700 couch might not fit in your next apartment. Stick with used or discarded furnishings until you buy a place of your own.

7. Don't hire a broker. Good deals can be found if you do the legwork yourself. And don't even look at Internet listings that carry a broker's fee, however tempting they may be.

change. Any change can come with enough determination and persistence. Just don't give up.

If a change is not possible, then your environment should not determine your happiness. Your outlook does. I didn't know I was living in what many might call an unsavory part of town. Even after I found out, I still enjoyed the unique characteristics, the interesting people, and the adventures and stories that came with it. I was in New York to grow, learn, and explore, and that's all that mattered to me. The rest was just gravy. I was willing to make sacrifices for the greater good of myself and my finances. I know that life does not take a predictable path. The best lives are lived by those who can adapt to any path.

AGE TWENTY-TWO
Checking account:
$9,000 (after the move)
Total net worth: $9,000

Chapter 2
Inspiration through Infomercials

WOW, *first hour of the day job. This sucks. A lot of paperwork. A lot of people who I just met are giving me orders. A lot of confusion. I'm supposed to be telling these people on the phone what, exactly? I've really got to learn the name of this company. First two calls are asking if we sell auto parts. I'm pretty certain we don't. I mean, I hope we don't, because I'm telling everyone we don't. My boss is too busy to talk to, so I'm just winging it until I get in trouble.*

"No, sorry, we don't have any auto parts. You sound like you are from the South. Are you from the South? Me too!" In my first thirty minutes, I learn that Richard Petty's last cup race was in Atlanta and that Mississippi's state beverage is milk. This job could actually be interesting.

Ahhhh, another caller. "You have a computer question?" Oh shit, computer question. There's no one to transfer this to? Where did everyone go? Okay, let's see how long he'll wait on hold. Damn, twelve minutes! Okay, buddy, I'll try to answer your ques-

tion. You want to do what? I have no idea what the words you're saying mean. Yeah, it's probably best you e-mail your questions in rather than calling.

Now, it didn't take me long to figure out that I didn't like having a day job. I think it took me about four hours. Right around lunch break, I was ready to quit. I was in New York, wanting to see New York, do New York things, and be a New Yorker. But I had to work eight hours *five days a week.* I couldn't believe this would be my life for the next forty years. Plus, I've never been good with authority, and, being the new guy, I was the subordinate to everyone. It sucked. I had to find a way to spend my days and make money that was better than being bossed around and told to do things I didn't want to do. I didn't want to rely on someone else for my financial security and definitely did not want to sacrifice my life for something I wasn't the least bit interested in—namely, computers. I just wanted to rely on myself and do what I wanted to do all day, every day. Maybe the rock-star/evil-genius thing was the way to go.

One night I found myself zoning in on a late-night infomercial. I couldn't get enough of watching a dozen millionaires with gigantic checks, bad hair, and three teeth explain how easy it was to be rich, young, and retired. I was transfixed. If they could do it, I could do it. There was no way these guys were smarter than me; they sounded like Jeff Foxworthy with a head injury. At least I understood that an oversized check fooled exactly no one. I watched the same commercial over and over and over again, looking for new nuggets of information on the secrets of their success.

I hoped that I could teach myself the secrets without buying the seminar, book, and audiotapes that were being pitched to me. Also, I knew there had to be a catch with anything priced $19.95. These hooligans had to be actors acting all *Hee Haw* to boost my self-confidence. Nevertheless, it was working, and I was mesmerized.

Once I mined every nugget of possible information from the infomercial, I decided I would teach myself the rest. I bought book after book after book about people who are rich and successful. I read biographies of millionaires, books about lifestyles of millionaires, and books written by millionaires (like this one!). What I learned from all my research was that there is no one way to be a millionaire. Millionaires come from all walks of life, and they all made a lot of money in a lot of different ways. But on the other hand, they all seemed to have a few things in common. I figured that if I also shared these traits, I too would have the tools to be a millionaire.

The common denominator that all the millionaires had was self-confidence, high self-esteem, and high personal motivation. (A high salary was usually par for the course.) They believed in themselves. And I mean *believed,* like New Coke believed. They had the self-confidence, on the border of delusional, that it took to be a millionaire. They thought they deserved better than the hand they were dealt. They believed that no matter how many times they failed, they would eventually succeed. And not marginally succeed, but be overly successful. They *believed* they would be millionaires before they became millionaires. They aimed high and didn't stop till they reached their goal.

I knew I had that in me. Being a millionaire started on the inside for these people, and once they were convinced on the inside that they were worthy, convincing the outside world didn't seem that daunting of a task to them. It sounded cheesy, maybe a bit New Age–y, but it seemed to be necessary to have the confidence to succeed. I decided to take it one step further. I thought on a bigger scale than all the millionaires I read about. They just wanted to be successful *eventually*. I wanted to be successful, specifically a millionaire, before I turned thirty. I had to force myself to have the same high self-belief as them. Right then and there I decided I wouldn't stop until I reached my goal, unless I got tremendous feedback from my peers that I was making a mistake.

Extreme Cheapskate Strategy

Carry a coin purse on your key ring. Yes, it's very grandfatherly, but it's also extremely helpful. You can pay for all your purchases to the exact dollar amount, thus putting more actual dollars in your pocket. It also gives you a place to put any loose change you pick up off the street. And having a bulky coin purse as a key chain makes losing your keys that much harder. One word of warning: Please adhere to the "212 rule." I've learned this rule by trial and error. Anything that is over $2.12 and paid for all in change will usually make the transaction last twice as long and piss off the cashier. If this doesn't bother you, feel free to break the rule. Unless I'm behind you in line.

Thinking big isn't enough—think humongous. It helped me find my goal of being a millionaire by thirty. I was twenty-two and so excited that I had something to shoot for, with a definite deadline. I was so jazzed that I had found my calling, I started telling everyone who would listen. My friends, family, and acquaintances all got to hear about my newfound mission, regardless if they wanted to or not. From everyone, I got these three reactions: At the beginning, it was usually complete disinterest. Eventually it would turn into an attempt to change my goal to something more "realistic." And lastly, the third phase was snickering. I couldn't believe they were snickering! I was trying to be a millionaire by thirty, not trying to make New Coke Mississippi's state beverage!

Now, their being disinterested in my goal was okay. I could handle that. As much as I wanted them to, my life choices didn't occupy the mind of everyone around me. I just called my friends uninformed ignoramuses when they attempted to change my millionaire goal to something more realistic like, say, trying to save $100,000 by thirty. I had the secrets of the rich; my research taught me the ins and outs of everything to do with millionaires. And I had the common denominator of all the other millionaires: incredible self-belief. I was just missing out on the huge income. But, of course, the majority of the reactions to my life's calling was just plain ol' snickering. My friends had laughed in my face! I had finally figured out what I wanted to do with my life, and this was a joke to them. I was personally offended. I just became more determined than ever to prove these unsupportive and negative people around me wrong. Some friends they were. I chose to be a millionaire by thirty to prove to myself that I could do it, but now I wanted to prove it to them too. It hurt, but I knew that in eight years I'd be thirty, and laughing not only last but the loudest (and the most pompously). I was already a millionaire on the inside, complete with the top hat, monocle, and oversized cigar. All that was left was being a millionaire on the outside.

ALAN COREY 101

Confidence is the key to success. To be a successful salesman, you need to truly believe in your product. Thinking like a millionaire means believing in yourself. You truly have to believe in that product, and go out and sell it to the world. If you feel like you are worth $100, you will probably make $100. But if you feel like a million bucks, you are one step closer to earning a million bucks. I find the healthier and more fit I am, the more confidence I have, not just about my appearance, but in all aspects of my life. Although I hate running and working out, when I'm done, I feel great the rest of the day. That great feeling turns into confidence, and it definitely carries over to all the other challenges in my life. Feeling great always makes things seem less daunting and more manageable.

Additionally, for some reason I keep an inner monologue in my head that just repeats itself over and over again. If I'm waiting for a bus, an elevator, or just killing time, I just start saying it to myself until whatever I'm waiting for arrives. I don't know where it comes from, and I don't know why I do it, but it definitely affects my approach to things. For about my first three months in New York, it was, of all things, a refrain of "I fucking hate shit." I don't know what it means, but I'm sure it was inspired by my day job. I would sing it over and over to myself, say it with different accents (most of them Spanish accents, thanks to my neighborhood), and it was always just stuck in my head like an earworm. I found my demeanor a little more aggressive, and I would be more stressed when I kept saying this crazy phrase, but I couldn't shake it out of my daily routine.

After I figured out my goal, I subconsciously changed "I fucking hate shit" to a more positive and less vulgar phrase: "I'm going to be a millionaire." And then I would start saying this to myself every day in my free time (walking to work, waiting in line, and so forth). After a while, I found myself more confident, less stressed, and more hopeful. Eventually, I started believing it myself. And it became such a routine thought in my head that it just seemed so natural to follow through with it. To this day, I still catch myself repeating phrases to myself when I'm waiting in lines. I've taught myself to instantly change my inner monologue if it is anything less than positive. It makes me a happier, more determined, and more confident person. You should do this too, no matter how much you fucking hate your day job's shit. (Just make sure you don't accidentally do it aloud, or you can forget sleeping with the hot girl in marketing.)

AGE TWENTY-TWO AND THREE MONTHS
Checking account: $10,000
Total net worth: $10,000

Chapter 3
Adult Education

WHAT *the hell is a 401(k)? The world's longest race? A pair of Levi's? I don't want to fill out all these forms. So this is what human resources does. Human resources people are apparently the kings of paperwork, but they sound like they should be spies for aliens. "Yes, our human resources have informed us of the Americans' plan to land on Mars. They are ninety light-years away. We must prepare." Oh man, more paperwork?!? I don't know if I want direct deposit; I don't think there are any ramifications for that. I'm not sure. Can't they just fill this out for me? How many dependents do I have? Do my roommates count? How about my fish? My bobbleheads?*

All of a sudden I was getting biweekly paychecks, and I didn't know what to do with them. I never had this kind of money before in my life. I didn't even know my options besides depositing them into a checking account. I wanted to get to the big leagues and be rich, but I didn't even know the rules to the game. With my forty-hour weekly reminder that day jobs suck and the pain of being laughed at by my friends for being ambitious, I had only one choice: I had to teach myself everything there was to know about money.

I bought and read everything on the subject. I read about stocks, real estate, bonds, mutual funds, 401(k)s, credit cards, retirement, and on and on and on. Some stuff I never did figure out no matter how many times I read it, but other things seemed to sink in right away. I soaked in as much as I could, and I felt even more confident to start down my millionaire path. I decided that if I didn't fully understand an investment, I wouldn't put my money into it. I knew ignorant investors made for broke investors. I also knew I had a lot more to learn, as I was currently both of those things.

Now, I did know one thing about finances. I knew my credit card was bad. Receiving a letter in the mail every month with "You Owe This Much" written in boldface type made it pretty obvious. So I decided to pay that off instantly and cancel my card. I was used to feigning interest in most things financial, but paying **interest** was a whole different story.

It made no sense to be paying fees just so some company could lend me money. If I had to borrow money to buy something, I just didn't need to buy it. No matter how cool my neighbors would think I was if I had a reggaeton ring tone, I could wait to purchase it with cash rather than credit. And if I could never come up with the cash, I could just record myself repeating the same word one hundred times and make my own annoying reggaeton ring tone. Either way, credit cards were out of the picture.

Next I got a savings account that went along with my checking account. I made sure not to get one that had a minimum-balance requirement. I never understood those: You get charged for being poor. That was definitely adding insult to injury, but it seems to be the standard. Usually, a savings account has a better interest rate than a checking account. Mine was the same. So I started putting as much in my savings as I could. The extra fifteen cents earned in interest were meager, but it was a start. I was earning my first interest ever, and it felt unnatural. I was being paid basically for depositing a paycheck in my savings account. The first time I saw that, I thought it was kinda cool. I thought, *okay, so this whole personal finance thing might be pretty interesting after all.* (It doesn't take much to get me excited.)

I expanded my research to cover **Roth IRAs** and index **mutual funds.**

Just being able to use those two terms in a sentence correctly made me feel rich. I liked that feeling. I couldn't wait to talk to someone at a cocktail party and say something cool about the differences between a Roth IRA and a **traditional IRA.** It would replace my party trick of hiding the party host's dog in the fridge.

And lastly, I figured out what the hell a 401(k) was.

And that I needed to learn. My company, like most, had this oddly named retirement plan and wanted to know if I was going to join. I was hesitant, though, because I didn't want to stay at this job until retirement; forty years of answering phones would put me in an insane asylum, probably where I'd have to answer more phones. Also, my company offered no match to any contribution I made to it. After questioning the HR alien, I learned that 401(k)s allow me to transfer my money to my next job and that it was still a good financial move, match or no match. So it still made sense to sign up for it. As long as the money is always mine, I might as well put it in a pro's hands to invest. Whenever I left 1-800-BORING, the money could go with me. I slowly but surely found my footing. I wasn't exactly krumping through the financial world, but I was learning to do the robot.

ALAN COREY 101

It pays to do your homework on all investments. Go to the library, check out books, or research online. You have to work hard to earn money, so be educated enough to make sound decisions on how to manage it. The best is to exhibit some self-control and not make purchases on credit. Wait till you have the money, rather than borrowing it to make most of your purchases. It's obviously more advantageous to earn money with interest than it is to pay money as interest. Get yourself in this **positive cash flow** situation as often as possible.

If you don't understand your company's retirement plans, meet with the human resources department. If you still don't know what they do, it's their job to explain your options to you. Ask a lot of questions, and invest only in something once you fully understand it. 401(k)s are always advantageous. Many companies will match your biweekly contribution, and that's free money. And unlike the situation I had with my mother, they are not allowed to cut it off unexpectedly. Take this perk and abuse it. Put in as much money as you can. Taking advantage of this is basically earning a bonus just for showing up to work each day. (Telling myself this at least made getting out of bed each morning a little more bearable.) Not only does this get invested for the rest of your life, but it also has the ability to put you in a lower tax bracket. (See 401(k) in the glossary.) A lower tax bracket means fewer taxes; therefore you have more money to invest. Index mutual funds and Roth IRAs are sound investments and should always be considered as a first place to invest any extra cash, especially if you have money sitting in a checking or savings account earning you less than 5 percent interest (and it probably is).

You can learn more about mutual funds at Web sites such as Morningstar (www.morningstar.com), Mutual Fund Education Alliance (www.mfea.com), and the Motley Fool (www.fool.com). Be sure to do your own homework, and talk to multiple sources before making any major financial decisions. Be sure to ask about all fees involved and be 100 percent sure that you understand everything about where you are investing your money. No one will care about your financial picture more than you, so be the squeaky wheel and get answers to all your questions.

AGE TWENTY-TWO AND SIX MONTHS

Checking account: $1,500

Savings account: $9,000

401(k): $2,200

Roth IRA: $3,000 (At the time, $3,000 was the maximum you could contribute in one year.)

Total net worth: $15,700

Chapter 4
Plastic Surgin'

FREE *T-shirt! I am going crazy for a free T-shirt! I don't even want this T-shirt. It'll probably shrink once I wash it, and it has a lame MasterCard logo on it, but I'm . . . still . . . filling . . . out . . . this . . . form. Why am I so compelled to get this shirt?? I can't stop. Okay, what do I have to do? Just sign up for this credit card, and it's mine. I don't want a credit card, I just want a free shirt. Okay, I'll make up my info. Okay, that looks like a legit address. Good, good, I'll just trick him. Make that up, and make that up. Wow, this is so easy. And . . . I . . . am . . . done. Okay, sir, here's your clipboard back. Yes, I'm sure everything is correct. What's my social security number? It's on the application. Oh, you want me to verify? I don't like to say it out loud; you know, identity theft and all. No, I swear it's my real number. Okay, I don't like saying my address either. Come on. Just give me the T-shirt. Yeah, well, you too. Your T-shirt sucks, and it wouldn't have fit anyway.* No, you have a good day, sir!

I got my first credit card right after college. It earned

me points at a gas station. I loved it, and it worked for me. Occasionally, I earned enough to get a free tank of gas. However, once I moved to NYC and became carless, my points became worthless. I canceled it and signed up for a new one, one where the allure of a free T-shirt tempted me so much that I actually filled out the forms with my correct information.

It was a music-based credit card, and by using it I could earn points toward music-related junk like a CD tower, a framed poster of a band, or I could even earn the original shirt they gave me free upon my application—in case I wanted another one. The credit card had a really high interest rate, but I didn't care because I was disciplined enough to pay off my balance each month, so it wouldn't affect me. When I finally received the card, I couldn't wait to go out and use it.

Extreme Cheapskate Strategy

Recommend your dentist, doctor, or other health specialist to everyone if you truly do recommend them. I turned my whole office on to my dentist and got her so many recommendations that she credited me $500 and a gift box of toothbrushes, dental floss, and toothpaste. I think if I'd asked her for free laughing gas, she'd have given me that too, but I needed my brain cells for now.

The first time I did use it was when my dad came to visit me and stayed in a five-star hotel right near Wall Street. I got there first, so I started checking him in. The hotel needed a credit card on file for incidentals, so I presented my flashy new credit card to the lady at the counter as if I were passing her the Hope diamond. I was proud and excited to start earning some points. The formerly sweet lady tried her best to contain her laughter. It was as if it were the funniest thing she had ever seen. I suppose she was used to corporate gold cards and had never encountered a juvenile credit card like mine, one emblazoned with the evidence that it helped earn points for crappy band gear. And it got me thinking that however rude this exchange might have been, I did have a freaking silly credit card. I was twentysomething, and I was collecting points for music knickknacks. And considering I didn't really *want* the stuff, it had to be the most pointless credit card for me ever. I decided that I should be earning necessities with my credit card, or, if that were not possible, at least earning my legitimate wants. I figured I should do some research and maybe get a credit card that came sans T-shirt.

I found out a couple of things looking for a credit card. It's not good for your **credit score** to continually change credit cards and roll over balances.

Longevity is the key to building good credit, and it is best to have only one or two cards and keep them for as long as possible (preferably one for life). All those Banana Republic and Gap credit cards will come back to haunt your credit score, so don't sign up for them, and forget about that one-time 10 percent discount. Secondly, I learned that no matter what credit card you have, you can usually lower your interest rate just by asking. The last thing a credit card company wants to do is lose a customer—even one who pays off the balance each month, because there's still a chance that person could get in trouble and miss a few payments. So being the Scrooge McDuck that I am, I found that just requesting a lower interest rate usually got it for me. All you need to do is call the hotline number on the back of your card, and the person on the other end usually will lower it for you. If not, just say that you found a card with a lower interest rate (which is usually not hard to do, and credit card companies know this). The threat of your leaving is so great, they will at least drop your interest rate half a percentage point. I do this every six months (around New Year's Day and then again on the Fourth of July), and over the past four years I have gotten my credit card's interest rate down to around 6 percent. I just want to make sure that if I do get in a situation where I owe money on a balance, it doesn't hurt me too much. Luckily, to this day, I've never carried a balance, nor have I ever wanted another credit card T-shirt.

I decided that the only necessity that I could earn from a credit card was money. The one I finally chose was easy to understand and easy to use, and its reward system was simple: For every $2,500 I put on my credit card, I would be sent a $50 **savings bond.** The only catch to the credit card was that I had to pay a yearly $50 fee to qualify for the rewards program. I did the math and figured I'd still be coming out on top. And just in case I ever did need to carry a balance, the card offered a midlevel interest rate. I got my credit card, put it in my wallet, and promptly forgot about it. I figured I would use it only in emergencies or when I found myself with absolutely no cash.

About a year later, I went to the mailbox, and in the mail was an official looking envelope. I thought I was being summoned or being called for jury duty. But inside was a brand-new, crisp $50 savings bond from my credit card company. I was thrilled! My own savings bond! I felt like Axel Foley's delinquent friend in the movie *Beverly Hills Cop.* It was so cool that I couldn't wait for it to happen again. And the only way that would happen again was if I charged more things to my credit card. Ah-ha, that's where they get ya! I came up with a plan that I don't think was that original, but it took some nerve, and it put the power of credit in my hands: I put every single bill I was getting on my credit card, every necessity purchase on my credit card, as well as just about any other expense I had. I started carrying no cash in order to earn more savings bonds. The only way I would get hurt with this plan was if I didn't pay off my balance each month, so the pressure was on even more to maintain enough in my checking account to cover my huge credit card bill that came every thirty days.

And it worked. I ended up earning nine savings bonds in a little over a year. I supplemented my income by almost $400 a year with this plan. Plus, I paid no interest and was charged only an annual $50 fee. I was earning points for myself rather than for some meaningless music accessory.

I continue to do this till this day, using the same credit card—this card is my lifer—and I still call the hotline on the back of my card every six months to try to lower my interest rate. The best part, though, is that the five-star hotels my dad stays at don't laugh at me anymore. Hopefully, this one credit card makeover is the only plastic surgery I will ever need.

ALAN COREY 101

If there is a gimmick involved (like free T-shirts), it usually means you aren't getting the best card available. Web sites such as Bankrate.com and Credit Card Goodies can usually lead you to the best reward cards out there. It pays to do research and find a card that fits your lifestyle. I still feel strongly that earning currency such as savings bonds or cash back is important in a card, as it can be redeemed easily if not instantly. It's optimal to find a card that you want to carry for the rest of your life.

Once you find the one that you want, cancel the rest. It's not merely enough to just not use the cards anymore, you have to actually call and close them. Checking your credit report, which you should do annually (it's free at www.annualcreditreport.com), will tell you how many cards are currently in your name and will give you information on how to close those accounts.

Annualcreditreport.com

There is also a way to log on and check your report for free every four months. There are three credit agencies: Trans-Union, Experian, and Equifax. All allow access to your report once a year from this Web site . Just check one agency's report, then four months later check another one, and four months later again for the last one. However, if you find an inaccuracy in any of the reports, it's probably best to check the rest instantly to make sure you get it fixed across the board.

Lastly, don't carry a balance. If you currently have a balance, prioritize and pay it off and stop adding to it. A credit card balance can be an expensive lesson in debt, and you can help yourself by calling and lowering your interest rate in case you ever get in a tight situation. Rather than having a credit card that you pay money to each month, make the credit card pay *you* money.

Getting your credit in check is also crucial. This will help you monitor against identity theft (you can see if an item has been falsely charged to you, if another card has been opened in your name, and so forth), keep your credit balances in line (did you forget about that old hospital bill, or the damn Gap card?!), and learn your entire financial history (that cell phone bill you never paid in high school might be on there). All of these steps are equally important. The Annualcreditreport.com site contains instructions on how to report inaccuracies, cancel old lines of credit, and pay off old debts that are eating up your credit score.

Your credit score determines how good a borrower you are, and it can affect you in many ways. It is a report card for lenders (lenders being people that will lend you money someday). Scoring over 700 will usually get you the best rates possible. A high credit score can get you a better car loan, mortgage rate, and credit card rate, which could save you hundreds—even thousands—of dollars a month if you have, say, a 709 score as opposed to a 648 score. You may not think it's a big deal now to make late payments on your credit card or any other bill, but it will come back to bite you in the ass when you're doing something you can't imagine yourself doing now—like buying a house—and those late payments from your bone-headed youth come back to haunt you. Also landlords and some jobs may access your credit report when doing a background check on you too. Remember, it's a score of your credit *history;* it's a lifetime score. And it can always be improved upon, so if it's low now, don't sweat it. Pay off the outstanding debts, cancel the cards you don't need, and fix any inaccuracies. And pick one lifetime credit card. It will save you tons of money down the road. It's best not to be surprised if any questions arise from a future lender you come across.

AGE TWENTY-THREE

Checking account: $2,300

Savings account: $9,400

401(k): $2,900

Roth IRA: $3,000

Total net worth: $17,600

Chapter 5
Excel-ing in Romance

WAIT *a minute, did she just make fun of my book collection? She said that these are the same books her dad reads. Did she mean that in a good way or bad way? I mean, her dad should have read these financial self-help books a long time ago, 'cause if he's starting to read these now, he's in trouble. She delivered it with such a weird inflection, though. Does she want me to offer her dad financial advice? No, wait, Tonya just seems perplexed by them. Does she think I'm a dad or something? I totally should tell her I don't have any kids. Wait, that's assuming that something's going to happen between us tonight. Whoa, if she respects her dad's taste in books, I must be so in. I'm like her dad away from home. Is that good? No, wait, I'm her dad away from home! I'm so out. Why did she have to say that? What's wrong with my books? Dates are so awkward!*

I did have a financial-self-help-book fetish. I wanted to learn what I had to do to become a millionaire, and I devoured everything I could on the subject. And each book, however boring it might have been to read, resonated on the same investing principal: The earlier you started a race, the sooner you'd finish. If I had started investing just one day earlier, I would be richer. Why didn't they teach me this on page one of every book? I don't know, but to be fair, I didn't mention it on page one to you guys, either. Hopefully for you it didn't take a full day to read this far.

Compound interest is the Tiger Woods of investing. The younger you start, the richer you'll be. I would have more money today if I had started just one day earlier. And if I'd started one month earlier, I would have been even further ahead, thanks to having an extra thirty days of interest compounded. It pained me that I didn't invest at least some in college a year earlier; I could have been so much further down my path to riches. As a result, I developed something of a love/hate relationship with compound interest. On the one hand, I was so happy to discover this power of making money, but on the other hand, I wish I had known about it so much earlier. Realizing that tortured me the same way it tortured me to realize the hot girl in high school used to want me. Too late now.

My income at the computer gig was $40,000 a year. It was a lot for most places, but in New York City it didn't go very far at all. That meant I didn't have much money to invest. I figured that if I couldn't control my income, I would still control my outflow—and outcome. I chose to reduce my expenses, scale back my lifestyle, and invest the difference in investments that earned compound interest: mutual

---

Extreme Cheapskate Strategy

Put everything on eBay before you throw it away. If someone bids, charge the normal price for shipping plus an extra dollar for "handling." Look to see if items similar to ones you regard as trash are already posted. If so, that means there is a buyer's market for it, and you might be able to sell it. It doesn't hurt to try to put up as much stuff as possible. A guy on the street once gave me about one hundred $1-off coupons for soy milk. I sold them on eBay (five sets of twenty coupons for $5 each) and earned $30 ($5 for handling) for five minutes of work. eBay is also a good place to get new high-end clothes and merchandise at a fraction of the price. Ted Baker, Betsey Johnson, Marc Jacobs, Banana Republic, J. Crew—they're all there.

---

funds, certificates of deposit (CDs), and even my savings account.

I decided that I would first cut down on my entertainment expenses, as that was where most of my money was going. I immediately went out to the store and bought a PlayStation for $300. This may seem backward to many, but my logic was sound. A night out in NYC cost me a minimum of $30 for dinner, cabs, muggings, or other miscellaneous expenses, but most often it came out to around $50. If I had an alternative form of entertainment instead of spending money out on the town, I could choose my PlayStation and save money in the long term. I was so determined to make this plan work, I kept a tally of how much money I was saving by being a homebody just once a week. In four months, the PlayStation saved me $640 I would have spent otherwise. Minus my initial $300 investment in the console, I had $340 extra to put in an interest-bearing account. It worked out perfectly. This is when my obsessive-compulsive disorder for saving money really began to sink in.

Now, I never did find a girl who wanted to spend a cozy night kicking my ass at PlayStation, but that doesn't mean my spartan lifestyle kept me from dating. I found that there were plenty of options for things to do that didn't cost a lot. I didn't date any women who required expensive gifts and $400 dinners, because that obviously wasn't happening, but I wasn't interested in that kind of chick anyway, millionaire or not. I had a hard enough time asking anyone out, much less someone who wanted a sugar daddy. Plus, I figured that if I really liked someone, and she really liked me, it didn't really matter what we did, because just hanging out would (hopefully) be a blast.

Still, some kind of activity is always nice, and here are some of the ways I got around spending buckets of cash while still managing to have some kind of dating life:

Museums: Many museums are free, and if they're not, they most likely have free days or hours. A quick trip to a museum's Web site will let you know when it lets people in gratis. Unless you plan to be an eccentric millionaire by thirty, don't go to a wax museum. Those are never free, and they, like your apparent taste, are a bit creepy.

Concerts: When the weather heats up, free concert series, often sponsored by the city or parks departments in most major cities, do too. There's tons of free—and, yes, good—music to be taken in. Ditto for outdoor movies. Plus, it makes you look like you've got your finger on the pulse of all the happenings in your city. You can learn about all of these in your local free news rags.

Art galleries: They're selling to really rich people, but it's free to look. And there's usually free wine and cheese on the opening nights of new artists.

Exercise: Take it however you want—running, walking, bike riding, Rollerblading, swimming at the public pool if it's not too gross, and so on. Take the initiative and show that you care about your health. You'll both finish the date feeling better about yourselves if nothing else.

Happy hour: Cheap drinks, and if you pick the right place, free food. Score, score, and, hopefully, score.

Parks and beaches: You've already paid for them with your tax dollars, so go ahead and use them. (I'm betting that one of you probably already owns a Frisbee.) Throw in a picnic while you're there. It's romantic, more or less stress free, but chances are high you might have to take your shirt off. Plan accordingly.

Games: Laugh if you want; many people will tell you nothing gets them going more than a steamy game of Scrabble. Double, triple, quadruple date option: Buy a few beers, invite people over, and have a Cranium blowout. Impress the ladies with your plate of handmade hors d'oeuvres. That's right: chips *and* salsa.

Cooking: While not free, it's a great way to have an awesome meal at a fraction of the price you'd pay in a restaurant. Case in point: Say you went out to eat and ordered two filet mignons, two salads, and a bottle of wine. The minimum you'd spend after tip would probably be about $100—and that's assuming you get the cheapest bottle of wine and tip 15 percent. Do it yourself, and you'd spend about $30. Filet mignon ($20) + wine ($8) + lettuce ($2). And believe me, cooking filet mignon is not a big deal—I've done it myself. (Well, I've watched someone less capable than me do it in my kitchen.) Obviously, you can cut this down even more by cooking pasta, but if you're trying to impress, you may want to go a bit more high end. A cheaper but still classy alternative for the non-steak-eater: Tilapia is way cheap and really tasty. So is veggie lasagna.

Volunteering: It's free, shows you give a damn about your fellow man, and leaves you feeling like a decent human being. Maybe you should do this solo sometimes too.

Cheaper movies: As I'll discuss later in this chapter, there are a lot of ways to skin this cinematic cat. Among them: Don't underestimate the power of matinees, as well as milking a subscription to a service like Netflix, or watching every free movie on demand through your cable service. My personal favorite is the turn-one-movie-ticket-into-three-movies trick. I can't tell you how it's done, but maybe you can guess. (I just strongly recommend choosing *one* of these options, and sticking to it.)

Mooch off your friends: Everyone is always doing something. Go see a friend's band, check out her improv show, or invite your date to come see *your* show. Usually fun, laid back, and could possibly earn you some date points if at the venue you find yourself on your friend's guest list.

Readings: If it seems like somebody's always hawking a book, it's because they are. (Yours truly coming soon to a bookstore near you.) Barnes & Noble, Borders, and your local independent bookstore all host authors doing free readings all the time. In a lot of cases, you can sign up to get e-mail notices of who's coming where, when. Literacy is sexy.

Rallies: Maybe you believe in the same causes—go represent together. Nothing says lasting memories like getting arrested together protesting politicians, taxes, and local library hours. Triple dating points if your protest works.

Flea markets/thrift stores/garage sales: While I generally discourage shopping as recreation, just rooting around in cool old stuff is fun, and if you happen to find a vintage

Lynyrd Skynyrd shirt for 25 cents, you have my blessing. (Although I'd probably sell it on eBay for a hefty profit.)

Street fairs: Free, often live music, perfect people-watching atmosphere. Instant good time.

Weddings: While not recommended for a first date, it certainly is a cheap one. Free food and open bar! Maybe kick in for a better wedding gift if you bring a guest, just to reward the newlyweds for getting your main squeeze loaded on someone else's dime for once.

TV tapings: If you live where a major television show is taped, there's a good chance you can get tickets for free. Especially game shows and dating shows. Check out the Web site to request them. Or befriend Chuck Woolery; I'm sure he could use the company.

Open houses: I'd be lying to you if I didn't include this one. Of course, it's one of my favorites, but not everyone finds this as scintillating as I do. Make a day visiting high-end homes for sale, just to see how the other half lives (or how you will live one day).

A final note on the dating front: It's important to remember that the person you're dating might also appreciate not having to break the bank to hang out with you. Living anywhere when you're in your twenties and making an entry- or midlevel salary is not easy (especially when you're trying to save money). And if you're a cool person—

that, as they say, is priceless. In other words: How much would you *not* pay to find someone you actually really liked and could spend more than five minutes with? Enough said.

With all this, I finally convinced a girl in New York to be my girlfriend.

Tonya loved movies. I thought movies were way too expensive to watch in the theater, and I had to make a stand. We could be patient and see every movie on TV for free in a few months or rent it from the video store a few weeks later, or bypass watching *Bridget Jones's Diary* altogether. Tonya took this as a personal affront, but she had an unhealthy compulsion for movies anyway. And I tried to cure her of this.

Tonya knew everything and anything about every film ever made, and had an impressive collection of DVDs to boot. Every word out of her mouth was a movie quote, a movie reference, or a movie factoid. This drove me crazy, but she was cute enough for me to overlook this one character flaw. But what really drove me crazy was seeing how much money she could have saved while maintaining her insane movie addiction. She wasn't *that* cute for me to overlook *this* major character flaw. All it would take would be a little effort on her part.

Extreme Cheapskate Strategy

In movie theaters that have unlimited popcorn refills, save your popcorn bag. My girlfriend and I used the same popcorn bag for about three months. Maybe a bit unethical, but desperate times called for desperate measures. And nothing is more desperate than eating a $7 bag of popcorn at a chick flick.

Tonya paid probably $50 a month for her premium cable access (HBO, Showtime, and so on). I know she also had Netflix, so that's $20 a month for someone to send her DVDs in the mail. Furthermore, she'd buy at least one or two DVDs ($15 each) a month. And then another $20 a month was spent going to movies, especially for an opening-night blockbuster, which was when she'd call me to be her escort. Anyway, that's $120 a month, or $30 a week, on movies alone! And she had just landed her first post-collegiate job, with a salary of $30,000.

Now, Tonya could really condense all her movie watching to one format like I did, whether it be only watching flicks on Netflix or only going to the movies during the matinee. But I knew that asking her to choose a single way to sate her movie jones would be the death knell of our relationship. So I proposed she eliminate just one source: the premium cable.

If she took the $50 a month she was spending on cable and invested it in the stock market, the results would be staggering. Through the power of Tiger Woods—er, compound interest—this is how Tonya's financial picture would have changed (not to mention her relationship with me): By altering her movie obsession just a smidgen and investing $50 a month her last four years in college, rather than paying for premium cable like she did, Tonya would have saved $2,817.49. And that's with a stock returning an average of only 8 percent. That's not bad, especially since she was still getting her movie fix in other mediums. But if she did this for a total of twenty years, she would have gained $29,451.02. For this kind of payday, I think Tonya could watch *Revenge of the Nerds II: Nerds in Paradise* at a friend's house.

But to take it one step further, let's trim Tonya's spending even more. If she did take my suggestion to watch movies only from Netflix, that would save her $100 a month. Investing that money in the same stocks as before would produce the following results, giving her over $100,000 in twenty-six years. (One note: This 8 percent return is over the long haul and not **timing the market** like some yahoos want to do.)

YEAR: BALANCE	
1: $1,244.99	15: $34,603.82
2: $2,593.31	16: $38,720.91
3: $4,053.55	17: $43,179.72
4: $5,634.99	18: $48,008.61
5: $7,347.68	19: $53,238.29
6: $9,202.53	20: $58,902.04
7: $11,211.33	21: $65,035.87
8: $13,386.85	22: $71,678.81
9: $15,742.95	23: $78,873.11
10: $18,294.60	24: $86,664.53
11: $21,058.03	25: $95,102.63
12: $24,050.83	26: $104,241.10
13: $27,292.03	
14: $30,802.25	

Tonya dumped me shortly after I presented her with this Excel spreadsheet. Granted, perhaps my tactic was a little much, but I was curious myself to see what she could have been earning with all of the money she was squandering. In the end, our approaches to managing our money were too extreme, and the relationship was stressed because of it. I was in a completely different mind-set from her, and I was determined to finish what I started. To be a millionaire by thirty, I couldn't be sidetracked because a cute girl was now making me go to the opening night of *Bridget Jones: The Edge of Reason* (no matter how aptly named the movie might have been).

ALAN COREY 101

The earlier you start investing, the easier investing will be for you. A mathematical formula known as the **rule of 72** demonstrates this.

The idea of saving $100,000 is overwhelming and sounds impossible. But the fact is that it's the exact same thing as trimming your spending by just *$25 a week*. It's not that hard to find that $25. Maybe you cut down on takeout, maybe you invite friends over for beers instead of heading out to a bar, and maybe you use your cell phone when the minutes are unlimited, or you get a cheaper plan. And, yes, it's cliché, but maybe you don't buy a $4 coffee every morning. If Tonya did that, after just ten years she'd have over $18,000, which could very well be a down payment on a house—lacking a down payment is one of the major reasons people can't afford to buy real estate. In my Excel spreadsheet scenario, Tonya's got it. But movies on opening night were more important to her. She had smoker's syndrome in this sense—she cared only about short-term gratification rather than the long-term effects of her actions while young.

Before every purchase, ask yourself: Can I do without this? Can this purchase wait till tomorrow? Can I find a creative work-around instead? Can I find it cheaper elsewhere? If you answer yes to any one of these questions, don't make the purchase. If you follow this internal monologue every time you pull out your wallet, your wallet will reward you.

Scale back your lifestyle as much as you can while

you're young, invest the money you would have spent otherwise, and compound interest will be your best financial friend—as well as a helpful tour guide down your path to being a millionaire.

AGE TWENTY-THREE AND TWO MONTHS
Checking account: $2,500
Savings account: $11,500
401(k): $3,700
Roth IRA: $3,000
Total net worth: $20,700

Chapter 6
Hail to the Cheap

OH, *I want to buy an iPod! Look at this, it's so tiny! And it's $200. I don't have $200! I mean, I have it; my ATM receipt says I have $2,500, and I've never had that much money before in my checking account. I can't believe I have $2,500 in my checking account! I'm so rich. I could totally afford this iPod and still have $2,300. Oh man, should I get this? Hold up, if I invested this $200, I could turn it into $215 by next year. And there will probably be an even better iPod next year. I should hold off. But I can't wait a whole year. Alan, there will be a smaller and better iPod next year. You know this. You can wait. Right, I won't buy it. I guess I'll just wait or ask for it for Christmas.*

Thanks to my breakup with Tonya, my entertainment expenses plummeted, and I decided I wanted to make cuts in other areas too. The hardest thing about this further belt-tightening was that it meant I had to get a grip on my impulse purchases. I needed to commit to buying only necessities (food, shelter, water) rather than wants (iPods,

Extreme Cheapskate Strategy

Many mobile phone companies give you thirty free credits each month for dropped calls. You have to call a 1-800 number and deal with an automated assistant to get credited for one minute. Call up to thirty times a month to get a total of thirty extra minutes of free phone time. It's worth it if you are continually going over by ten to fifteen minutes each month and don't want to upgrade to a more expensive plan. It's also a good stress reliever: Instead of counting to ten when you're upset, just make ten phone calls to the robot operator. You'll stop stressing over your problems, as you can now take it out on the automated person on the other end of the line.

beer, more beer). When I categorized every purchase as either being a "necessity" or a "want," I realized I could cut down my expenses tenfold if I bought only what I truly needed.

The hardest part was looking at my ATM receipt and seeing that I could afford something, then trying to talk myself out of buying it. I figured that if I wouldn't give an alcoholic access to my liquor cabinet, I shouldn't give someone trying to save access to money. I had to make it so that I couldn't get to my cash.

So the next day I opened up a second bank account at a different bank across town and transferred all my money in my current savings account to it. I intentionally chose one that was inconvenient for me to get to. Afterward I went into work and went back to human resources. I needed some automatic assistance to implement my new "out of sight, out of mind" strategy to investing. I told HR to direct deposit 40 percent of my paycheck each month into my new inconvenient bank account. I purposely didn't memorize the number of the new account, and I instantly threw away the ATM/debit card that came with it. In short, I took away my access to almost half of my income. This extreme measure meant only one thing: I was now officially bat-shit insane. I didn't even want to know how much money I had in there, ever.

On top of that, I asked HR to sign me up for my office's 401(k). The legal maximum I could contribute was 15 percent of my paycheck. 1-800-SNOOZE didn't have any company match (a common practice at many companies), but I put the full amount in anyway. At this point, I was forcing myself to live off 45 percent of my income. These were drastic moves, especially in an expensive city like New York, but I was determined, and fully immersed in my financial OCD, so I didn't stop there.

After meeting with HR, I realized that I would have to invest on my own as well. My job was only going to get me so far. So I went online and opened up a **brokerage account.**

I had to start investing in mutual funds, so I opted for a run-of-the-mill index fund. I set up an automatic transfer of $100 every two weeks from my original bank account to my mutual fund. That put me in another $200 bind each month (another 6 percent of my salary). After all the constraints I put on my paycheck, I'd whittled my $40,000 yearly salary down to $15,600 a year, or 39 percent of my salary. And this was before taxes were taken out. I was forcing myself into poverty, relatively speaking, for Manhattan. Most people thought I was off my rocker, but as I saw it, I had no choice. I didn't have the skills or the experience necessary to get a high-paying job, so if I wanted to save, I had to live on as little as possible.

> **Tip:** Yes, some big-money corporations deplete the environment of valuable resources or make their money using unethical business practices, but if you don't agree with them, there are several brokerages that employ socially responsible investing. Feel free to invest in these.

One positive effect of all this insanity was that it put a complete stop to all my impulse purchases. Whenever I bought something, it was a very carefully considered decision. My inner monologue would just repeat, *Do I need this, or do I want this?* Anything I wanted, I refused to purchase. I was on such a tight budget, if I did buy something I simply wanted, I wouldn't have been able to afford anything I absolutely needed. No matter what, all purchases were intensely scrutinized.

Once I started buying necessities on a budget, I was forced to comparison shop. I learned that buying food in bulk was advantageous, but only as long as I could eat everything I bought in bulk before it spoiled. Plus, comparison shopping all my food purchases helped me pinpoint all the product-placement nuances of my grocery store. Anything at eye level or placed near the checkout counter was priced at a premium. I figured that the manufacturers of these products paid extra to have their items in this zone of shoppers' impulse buys. So I began buying things requiring the bending of knees or the assistance of an employee to get something off the top shelf. It was a little extra work, but I needed to save every single penny, and the cheaper stuff was always a bit harder to reach. I was on a treasure hunt. Granted, it was a treasure hunt for generic-brand peanut butter and knockoff Cheerios, but a treasure hunt nonetheless. It was obviously in the grocery store's best interest to put the most expensive stuff within easy reach, and I wasn't falling for it.

After about two weeks, I was used to my new budget. It almost felt like I was back in college again—I was eating cheap food and drinking a whole lot of water. This time, though, I was drinking water to be thrifty, not to cure a hangover. In addition, I benefited from living in an area surrounded by cheap take-out restaurants. (I ordered take-out often—never delivery—to avoid paying a tip.) I can't say enough about ordering vegetarian takeout, the cheapest route every time.

Trying to find the cheapest food sources was my way of becoming a modern-day hunter-gatherer. One day, I found a way to get heavily discounted baked goods. I located a bakery that boasted a Baked Fresh Daily sign in the window. I knew if they baked goods daily, there had to be some baked goods that were a day old and, hopefully, sold at a discount. I walked in at closing time, and, sure enough, they were about to toss a bunch of bagels and croissants into the trash. I asked for them, and they gave them to me for free. The next day I came back, and they gave them to me for free again. The next day I came back, and they charged me half price. *WTF?* I paid it, and from there on out it became half price for me. I was still going back, though, as a half-priced bagel with a dollop of peanut butter from my industrial-sized jar back home made for a hearty dinner on many nights. Now, that's cheap!

Extreme Cheapskate Strategy

Never buy bottled water. It's unnecessary. Go to any fast-food joint and get a free cup of water that's twice the size of a bottle of water. Bonus: it's iced. The bottled-water business should be successful only in third-world countries. People, we live in America; take advantage of it. And if you need some flavor, load up your cup with free lemons and artificial sweetener for some bargain ice-cold lemonade.

The ultimate meal for saving money, however, is no secret to many: ramen noodles. I discovered that if I bought a
six-pack of ramen noodles for 99 cents, I would have a
16.5-cent lunch every day. If I bought a twenty-four-pack,
it came down to 13 cents a day. Food was a necessity, but
getting it didn't mean I had to splurge. I admit, it wasn't
the healthiest maneuver, but I ate ramen noodles for lunch
for three straight months. To this day, I can't even smell the
noodle soup without getting nauseous, but for those three
months it was the best smell I'd ever experienced. Why? It
was the smell of dollar signs accumulating in my bank account, and it helped keep my food budget to around $2 a
day *every single day.* What was wrong with me? After a
while I got used to it, so much so that I stayed on this
measly food budget for two and a half years. I don't think
I'd ever been that skinny in my life, but I was also never
richer in my life, either. With my extremely limited access
to money, I was forced to get creative and prevent myself
from buying unnecessary wants. And it made me comparison shop for my necessities. Both played major roles in
helping me save enough to begin my millionaire journey.

ALAN COREY 101

If your money is inaccessible, you can't spend it. I went
to great lengths to have my money hidden from me and to
have it automatically invested. I was benefiting twice by (a)
forcing myself to live on a budget and (b) taking advantage

of **dollar cost averaging** through my online brokerage account.

And the best part was, I didn't have to do anything except spend thirty minutes in the human resources office and thirty minutes online. After that, it was all about keeping my impulses in check.

Resisting the temptation to buy things you simply want is incredibly hard, but if the alternative is not buying the things you truly need, you stop caring so much about splurging or buying yourself that occasional present. Treat yourself when you are a millionaire rather than when you are just starting out. Trust me, the presents are much better.

If you take a look at how you spend your money, you'll probably find that most of it goes to food, entertainment, and transportation. Entertainment is the easiest to scale back. Just be disciplined and choosy on how much paid entertainment you allow yourself each month. For transportation, the best ways to go are subways, buses, walking, and carpooling. These alternatives to a car or a cab will save you money, and they're also good for the environment.

One last super-low-budget food option is Alan's Stick-to-Your-Ribs Breakfast Blend. It's actually a recipe created by one of my best friends, Katie, to help me adhere to my $2-a-day food budget.

INGREDIENTS:

Dry oatmeal

Raisins

Milk

The trick is that it's not prepared like normal oatmeal. Just buy a big ol' container of oatmeal and treat it like dry cereal. Put it in a bowl, add raisins and milk, and serve cold. You now have a wonderful cereal-like concoction that tastes better than store-bought Raisin Bran, and it's also more filling. Plus, it's much, much cheaper. You can buy a large container of dry oatmeal and a large container of raisins for under $4 combined, and this can easily last two or more weeks. I ate it for dinner many times when I was sick of having industrial peanut butter and half-priced bagels.

AGE TWENTY-THREE AND FOUR MONTHS
Checking account: $2,500
Savings account: $0
Second, hidden savings account: $?
401(k): $4,000
Roth IRA: $3,000
Mutual fund: $1,000
Total net worth: $10,500 + hidden amount ($11,500, which I took from my savings account and put into my new account to prevent access to it) = $22,000

PART II

Estate of Affairs

Chapter 7
Getting Real (Estate)

WOW, *it's almost been one year of insane saving. I'm about to turn twenty-four, and the past year actually flew by and wasn't so hard after all. It's New Year's. I should make this my annual check on finances and see how I've been doing. I'll have to head across town today and see what I have in my checking account. Maybe I'll have enough to buy real estate. In all those books, it said to buy real estate, but I'm not exactly sure what that entails. I should buy an apartment. Okay, I will check my balances first and then figure out what to do. I hope I can buy real estate—that would definitely sound a lot cooler than 401(k)s when I'm schmoozing at cocktail parties. I want to talk about an apartment I own. Okay, that would be bragging. But it still would be fun! Yeah, bragging is fun. Okay, maybe I'll just buy a bunch of real estate and write a book about it. I'll wait to brag then. Way cooler. Bragging in a book would be the best. I'd call it* A Million Bucks by 30!

It felt great to check my balances in all my accounts

after one year. At the age of twenty-three, I had a pretty decent **portfolio.** I was definitely ahead of my friends who weren't saving, and I was way ahead of where I had been financially just one year earlier. I couldn't believe I was able to save money while living in one of the most expensive cities in the world. It took some work, but now I could see it was actually paying off. I had $11,500-plus in my hidden bank account. It felt good to have that.

My portfolio was very heavy in stocks too, which is fine when just starting out when you're young. Even though stocks are risky in that you could lose some money, a long-term investment timeline enables you to weather the ups—and inevitable downs—of the market. I figured I could take some of my most **liquid** money and either buy more stocks or maybe even buy a place to live. Real estate seemed attractive to me, and that $11,500-plus sitting in my hidden savings account was earning me very little, but at least I didn't have access to spending it. I needed to branch out, but what could I buy with around $12,000 in the bank? I mean, besides a wonderful week in Vegas.

To find out, I started looking at apartments. I remembered the no-money-down deals from the infomercials, but they seemed a little sketchy. Even I knew that if I put no money down, I'd end up with a gigantic **mortgage** and have a huge monthly payment because (a) I'd owe more money and (b) putting no money down meant that I'd be charged a higher interest rate. So I figured I'd rather make a small **down payment,** get a better interest rate, and therefore have monthly payments that were a little bit more manageable.

If I could find a place in New York City for $100,000, I would be able to put down 10 percent ($10,000), and instead of paying rent, I'd be paying off my own place each month. That sounded way better than forking over my money to a landlord every month and never seeing it again. It all made sense, but, of course, there was one catch: I had to find a place for $100,000 in New York City.

I scoured the Web, the newspaper, and listings at realty companies. Everything within my price range was in New Jersey or the farthest commute possible from the far reaches of Brooklyn. I didn't care what neighborhood it was in; I just wanted to be within a thirty-minute commute of my day job. The truth was, the day job was growing on me; the people were cool, the hours were flexible, and I liked the steady paycheck. Sure, it was boring, but it didn't require me to wear a tie, and that went a long way with me. I figured that I would stay there one more year and then really find my way. The evil genius/rock star might just still be in me yet. (I'd also read that having a steady job could help you get a mortgage, so I was staying put.)

I saw a one-bedroom apartment that I really liked in the Murray Hill neighborhood of Manhattan for twice my budget. However, I couldn't make things tighter financially than they already were. I saw a tiny, decrepit shamble of a place in Dumbo, Brooklyn, that was way overpriced, and the Realtor reinforced several times that the owner wasn't going to budge on price, so I moved on. And I went to many **open houses** in places that were way out of my league locationwise (and, therefore, pricewise), but I just wanted to get comfortable with the open-house process and pick up on what types of questions other people were asking.

I felt like a fish out of water, and I looked at these trips as my vocational school, just by eavesdropping on savvy buyers' comments and concerns. I finally found a one-bedroom apartment listed for $110,000 and went to the open house. I was the only one who showed up. The apartment was in Clinton Hill, a transitional neighborhood of Brooklyn—more about that in a bit—but this was also an area filled with beautiful historic brownstones and tree-lined blocks. I figured that **transitional neighborhoods** were a good place to start investing, as the property values in these areas tend to increase faster than those in already established neighborhoods. I would be buying in a "bad" neighborhood, so to speak, but I took an educated risk that in a few years I would own a property in a good one, where people would want to move.

Extreme Cheapskate Strategy

You never have to buy an umbrella. When it's raining, just walk into any restaurant or grocery store and ask to see its lost and found. Explain that you lost your black umbrella, and they'll bring you a box of twenty. (Every lost and found has a minimum of twenty black umbrellas.) Now, don't feel guilty. When you are done with it, leave the umbrella at another restaurant or grocery store. It's a bit like recycling, and it's good karma too. We could dry up the umbrella business if we worked together on this.

The reputation of this particular neighborhood the last twenty years was one of crime and drugs. However, it seemed like the pendulum was swinging back toward improvement for the neighborhood as a whole. I could tell by the new stores popping up in the neighborhood, new renovations happening to other houses on the block, and new people moving in. It was close to public transportation. A nearby park was just starting to get cleaned up by local volunteers. Neighboring areas were getting too expensive for moneymaking business folk, so I figured they would have to settle for this area if they wanted to buy. I believed that the neighborhood's bad period had definitely peaked, and it was getting primed for a renaissance. And besides, it had to be safer than the projects, right?

But as cheap as the apartment was, the price was still too high for me. I was especially excited about the place because the next cheapest apartment I saw was listed for $135,000, and I knew there was no way I could afford that. If I wanted that one, I would have to wait another whole year to save more money, and by then the asking price would most likely be even higher.

The place for $110,000 was small, and the bathroom needed a complete makeover, but the ceilings were high and the building was nice too. If I was going to buy, it would have to do, because that was all I could afford. In the end, I realized that the only way I could afford the place was to put in a **lowball offer** and try to get it for under $100,000.

The fact was that I had nothing to lose: Either they would take my offer and I'd buy it, or I'd hunker down and wait another year. So I called up the real-estate agent who had shown me the apartment the week before. I told her that I wanted to put in an offer of $90,000 and would put down 10 percent. My strategy was simple: I was hoping that she'd split the difference, and we would come to an agreement of $100,000. I knew they were still scheduling open houses trying to get bids from other people, but when they came back three days later with a counteroffer of $105,000, I could tell that no one else was bidding on the place. But the price was still too high for my meager savings, so I came back with another offer of $95,000 in an attempt to get her to split the difference once again. This went back and forth a few times until her lowest offer was $101,000 and my highest was $99,000. After I refused once again to go into six digits to buy the place, she finally counteroffered with $99,600. I accepted it. I couldn't believe it—I was buying an apartment in New York City! (Well, Brooklyn, which is technically part of New York City. I did something good is what I'm getting at!)

The whole process of buying a home was pretty expensive, and the costs were more than I anticipated. Every state is different, but in New York I had to pay an attorney, taxes to the state, and other fees. You are required to receive a **good faith estimate** when you apply for a mortgage, and should you buy property, it's important to look at this carefully, because it will outline all the miscellaneous fees that come with a **closing**.

It's important to know that when you buy real estate, you don't just need money for a down payment and your monthly mortgage, but you also need a chunk of change to pay all of the fees that will allow you to pay that mortgage in the first place. There are transfer taxes, recording fees, transfer fees, and more. Get estimates on all these up front from your lender. When I walked out of the closing with my new keys in my hand, I felt broke, because as far as liquid cash, I kind of was. However, my portfolio had a brand-new look to it. My checking account reflected $700, but on closer inspection I could see that real estate was already making me richer. I would just have to replenish my checking account and my newly exhausted hidden savings account once again. (Check out my net-worth tally at the end of the chapter if you can't see the full picture.)

I definitely came out on top with this real-estate purchase. The $11,300 I spent at the closing earned me $19,400 in **equity**. Equity is the difference between what a person owes on a property and what it's worth. For instance, the apartment was worth $110,000. The owner agreed to sell it to me for the lower amount of $99,600. I put down a

$9,000 down payment at the closing and got a $90,600 mortgage from the bank. That meant I owed $90,600 on a place worth $110,000, which gave me $19,400 in equity.

So here's the math: $90,600 mortgage + $19,400 equity ($9,000 down payment + $10,400 lower price) = $110,000.

Equity is the least liquid of capital, but I wasn't planning on needing that $19,400 any time soon. I just hoped I didn't have any trouble covering my new mortgage payments. I got a thirty-year mortgage, which required me to pay $700 a month, and my apartment came with a $400-a-month maintenance fee for the superintendent, insurance, and a doorman. To be honest, I wasn't sure if I was going to be able to handle the huge leap from paying a rent of $400 a month in the projects to shelling out $1,100 a month at my new place. To make things extra tight, I still planned to keep on living off 39 percent of my salary. But I was determined to make it work somehow. In the back of my mind, the issue of potentially putting myself in a precarious financial situation wasn't going to happen. I could always stop living off such a small percentage of my salary to make ends meet if necessary. Luckily, I got a raise at work to $42,000, which came with a $5,000 bonus. Things would work out, at least for the short term.

How to Sniff Out a Good Deal

If you're serious about buying your first place, here are some key strategies to finding a great deal:

- Identify transitional neighborhoods where other people are investing. Look for retail and housing development, as well as existing services such as grocery stores or transit hubs, which will help draw people to an area.

- Consider buying directly from the owner. It's more complicated and more work, but it can also save you thousands in fees and may help you get a better price, especially if the seller doesn't know the market and has undervalued their property.

- Be open to an apartment with potential. If it seems like you could make improvements and greatly increase the value of a place, you may have found a diamond in the rough. You don't have to make changes right away, but you can if you decide to sell.

- Know the market. It's crucial to understand the value of similarly priced properties; this will help you know if the asking price is way too much or, ideally, too low.

- If you're in love with a place, and cannot afford it, one way to save money is to submit a lowball offer. Or negotiate that the seller pays closing fees or will install an appliance or two. (Obviously, this works only if the seller is desperate to unload, or you're in a buyer's market. If you've done your research, you should have a pretty good sense of the current climate.)

- Consider borrowing money from your parents or friends. If it's an option, it's a good one. Parents are usually not so keen on financing your trip around the world for the hell of it, but they know that property is an investment and may be open to helping you take this big step. Friends, especially those with money, know this too.

- Consider putting down 10 percent. This is not an ideal situation, as it means that you'll pay more over the long term for your mortgage—and it often carries additional fees, like mortgage insurance. But having 20 percent of the purchase price in hand is not always essential, nor is it always financially possible. Get the best you can get for what you have, and the investment, if done correctly, will always work out for you.

ALAN COREY 101

The power of equity in real estate is tremendous. It's money that is the least liquid; therefore it's the hardest to spend on something frivolous. And, historically, real-estate values tend to go up over time, turning your equity into even more equity. To get the fastest return on real estate, it's usually best to invest in property in a changing neighborhood. But remember, real estate is a long-term investment. Buy a place that you want to live in for a while and be patient waiting for the neighborhood to change around you. If you don't have a ton of money to buy a place in the best part of town, turn your attention to neighborhoods on the cusp of change for the better. Look for signs that people care about the area, like local community programs working hard to clean up where they live. Consider the practical aspects of what makes a place livable. Is there a supermarket nearby? If applicable, is mass transit accessible? Is there a park or good schools in the area? Do you see development, even in its most early stages, cropping up? All of these things will draw other people to the neighborhood, because they make an area a desirable place to live. And as more people move in, more conveniences will move in too, and before you know it, you're no longer in a cusp area, but maybe even in one of the hottest parts in town. Regardless, your property value—and equity—has gone up.

It's also important to remember the power of low-balling in real estate or in any other negotiating situation. Just because someone has an asking price doesn't mean that he won't take less. Never walk away from a deal you think you can't afford. It doesn't cost anything to put in an offer, so throw it out there. In real estate, you'll usually be using a real-estate agent as a go-between, so you won't have to deal with an irate seller. Besides, he'll either take your offer and accept it, counteroffer, or just ignore it. Just remember that you never know the situation on the seller's end: He may be moving, already have bought another house, or need some quick capital and be willing to go down in price to get it. One thing is true: You'll never know if you never try.

AGE TWENTY-THREE AND ELEVEN MONTHS

Checking account: $700

Savings account: $0

Second, hidden savings account: $4,200 (spent $11,300 of it on the closing and then deposited most of my bonus money back into it)

401(k): $4,500

Mutual fund: $2,400

Roth IRA: $3,000

Equity: $19,400

Total net worth: $34,200

Chapter 8
Splitting Lairs

I can't believe I actually own something of value. My PlayStation was the most expensive thing I had ever bought, and now one year later I've purchased a piece of property! So this is the American Dream, huh? Owning property. It feels pretty cool, but damn, this is one expensive dream; it's costing me a shitload each month. And this is one hell of a lonely dream; I see why most people wait till they have a family to buy a house. I hate living by myself! I'm boring myself to tears here. I have no one to yell at. Who's going to entertain me? This place is too quiet!

I was driving myself nuts in my new place. I had never lived by myself before, and I learned quickly that I hated it. It was lonely coming home to an empty house every day, and I was bored. It wasn't a dream come true at all, and it started to drive me crazy that I was paying $1,100 a month for a place I wasn't truly enjoying. I needed to make a change in my living situation, and fast.

I looked the place over and realized that my living room was just a waste of space. Whenever I was home, I was in my bedroom eating dinner on my bed while watching TV. I hadn't used the living room at all during the first two months I owned the apartment. The space was just a storage area for a couch I found on the street, a table I pulled off the curb, and a lamp that was left behind by the previous owner. I realized the unused space would make for a great second bedroom, which I could rent out to earn some extra money. All it would take was a heavy curtain and some ceiling hooks, and I'd have a space that surely *someone* would be game to live in. I made my "renovations," and after sending out a few e-mails, a friend was ready to move in a week later. Sure, now the apartment didn't have a living room, but that wasn't so unusual in many tiny New York apartments, and I obviously wasn't going to miss having one. Not only that, but I was going to charge my friend only $400 in rent, and you really can't argue with that kind of deal. Hell, I dodged bullets for it at my first place. But with this new arrangement, I killed two birds with one stone. I reduced my living expenses by offsetting my maintenance fees with my rental income, and I had someone around to talk to whenever I was bored. The American Dream, or at least *my* American Dream, was alive and well after all.

Having someone pay me money just because I owned some walls and a ceiling opened up something of a Pandora's box. I loved it, and I couldn't wait to purchase another place and do it again. And I figured that if I bought a place that was bigger, with more rooms, it could earn me even more money. People would always need a place to live, especially in New York, and if I could buy more property, I could keep renting to more people! It was brilliant! But so simple! I felt like Donald Trump must have felt after his first real-estate venture, but I had normal hair.

Extreme Cheapskate Strategy

Libraries are not just for term papers. You can check out for free many of the latest bestsellers in books, DVDs, and CDs. Your tax dollars are paying for it, so take advantage of it. It's also good to know where all the public libraries are in case you ever have an urgent need to use a bathroom out in public. (Librarians are much friendlier than Starbucks employees.)

But I was thinking too far ahead again—after all, I didn't really have any cash to do such an adventure. I would have to save up for another down payment, or borrow some more money, and once again see what I could afford. But this plan seemed like a viable way to reach my goal of being a millionaire, and I figured that if I could add just one property every year, it could very well be my winning ticket. In the short term, I had to be happy with my very small-scale real-estate "holdings": my two-bedroom with no living room and a fabric curtain for a wall. But I knew where I was headed and what I had to do: keep saving as much as I could and start preparing to make my next deal.

ALAN COREY 101

Be adaptable and open to revising your plan, and see opportunity in those revisions. I'd finally accomplished one of my major goals, and when I got there, I realized it wasn't all it was cracked up to be. I was paying way more than I wanted to (or could afford, given my self-imposed budget restrictions), and the fact was, I was bored and lonely and needed to make some changes.

I came up with a way to improve both situations by adding an extra bedroom, and my willingness to adjust my plan left me much happier.

Also, you should actively seek out opportunities to generate extra income and be willing to downgrade your lifestyle. Part of the secret of being a power saver is living below your means and making sacrifices. Often, it's possible to generate more income by making sacrifices.

I could have lived in my extra space in my apartment, but there was no need. I actually enjoyed having someone else around, and it knocked $400 off my monthly expenses. If I'd had a garage, I would've rented that out to a neighbor with too many cars. If I'd had a basement, I would have rented it out to kids needing a band space. If I'd had a backyard, I would have rented it out too (not sure who would rent a yard, but, then again, I'm sure someone would). This is called *passive income.* You earn money for not doing any work. Find things you own or have access to, and make some money from them—they may be things you won't even miss.

Find what you have that is of value to others and make some money from it, whether it's a shed, a parking space, or an unfinished basement. It may seem basic, but you should always be looking for opportunities to lower your expenses and increase your income as much as possible. More money in, less money out; it's one of the most effective ways to become a millionaire by thirty.

AGE TWENTY-FOUR

Checking account: $3,400

Savings account: $0

Second, hidden savings account: $?

401(k): $4,600

Mutual fund: $2,600

Roth IRA: $3,000

Equity: $19,400

Total net worth: $33,000

Chapter 9
Getting Testy

OKAY, *let's see what we have here. All right, a check for $1.50! Oh, oh, what's inside this one? $6! Jackpot! I've been good, but not this good. Next envelope, what do we have? Oh damn, phone bill for $35. Whammy. Come on, Alan, big bucks. No whammies. Next letter is . . . a check for $10! Oh yeah! Okay, one more envelope to go . . . and it looks like a bill, and I don't want to open it, but it's the rules . . . unless . . . it's . . . for . . . my roommate—and it is! All right, Alan walks away with a sigh of relief and negative $17.50 after today's exciting game of Mailbox Roulette. Come back tomorrow to see if Alan will finally have what it takes to win or watch him die trying. Thank you to our sponsors Sprint, random lab test, and survey. This emotional roller coaster was provided by the U.S. Postal Service.*

Being supercompetitive, I like turning everything into a game. I invented a game of "How Cheap Can I Go?" to challenge myself to be as thrifty as possible. Each day I tried to outdo myself from the previous day's spending total. I would get completely bummed out if I lost, so I did everything in my power not to lose. Its counterpart was "How Much Can I Make?" where I would see how much money I could make away from my day job. Naturally, combining the two games became Mailbox Roulette. (I never said I wasn't geeky.)

Although I had a new roommate and was making more money, I knew it wasn't going to be enough to reach my goal of being a millionaire by thirty. I had to give it my all in making as much as I could *and* saving as much as I could. I could ask for a raise at work only every year or so, so I had to come up with some extra ways to supplement my income. I became addicted to finding other sources of what I saw as easy money to pay off annoying but necessary expenses like my phone bill, electric bill, or subway card. Luckily, I found that offering myself up as a guinea pig was a great way to bring in some extra cash. It was so amazingly rewarding for me to pay off an entire phone bill from seven different checks that my desire to make more money on the side increased even more.

My sister, a psychology grad, turned me on to earning small payouts for participating in research studies. Bulletins looking for volunteers to participate in research groups and focus groups were often posted in her classrooms. These studies needed to film people doing puzzles, taking tests, or figuring out a riddle with a group. They usually took twenty minutes and paid $10. Not bad, and you could do as many as you wanted. You just had to be willing to be a human guinea pig, and I saw no harm in that. These tests were offered every month or so, and my sister would notify me when there was a new one posted on campus—she actually participated in many of them herself.

Her big payday from this was for a test on brain activity and husbands. She earned $200 for getting a CAT scan while holding her husband's hand, and then again when she wasn't holding his hand. It took four hours; that isn't too bad just to be uncomfortable, stationary, and holding a loved one's hand. Her husband got loot too, so it was a win-win for him. (Actually, *especially* for him, as he didn't have to get a CAT scan and wasn't allowed to talk to her.) After hearing about his lucky payday, I had to find opportunities to do these things more often, rather than wait around for more postings in my sister's classroom.

I ended up finding Web sites of companies that did similar work; they would pay me to take tests, fill out surveys, and try products for cash.

Websites that can help you make a few extra bucks: www.greenfieldonline.com, www.pineconeresearch .com, www.online-sweepstakes.com, www.your2cents.com, www.testspin.com, www.surveyspot.com.

I made some extra dollars doing quick and easy things like talking to a stranger on the phone for ten minutes as part of a dialect study, being filmed taking a test on pop culture, and trying different types of deodorant for a week and giving my feedback. (With that last one, I came out on top: free deodorant, no stinky pits, and cash! Okay, honestly, my coworkers and roommates might have come out on top, but still, *someone* was benefiting.) I even turned down some gigs, as in the end, sometimes time *is* money. I was financially determined, but a three-hour survey on washing machines for $5 was not enough to secure my guinea-pig services.

One of my best friends, Paddy, was my chief rival in this game, and he was the king of securing odd jobs to supplement his income. He was a grad student, and he turned down nothing. He would always top my war stories with his own, and ours became another love/hate relationship. I was definitely cheaper than him, but his strength lay in procuring side gigs. He did so many focus groups and surveys, he ended up getting a job at a place conducting them. Not even counting the fact that every one he found somehow came with a free lunch, he even usually beat me based on the "no-effort factor" alone. His crowning glory came when he landed *a slipper testing* gig. A reputable firm would send him really expensive slippers each week, and he'd have to wear them an hour a day and give his feedback. He'd send in his report, keep the slippers, and then wait for his paycheck to arrive. A few weeks later, he would wrap up the slippers and give them out as Christmas presents to his family, earning/saving him a several-hundred-dollar bounty for a few short walks around his apartment.

> **Tip:** Never buy a brand-new car. A car loses 20 percent of its value the first *day* of ownership. Let some flashy trendsetter take that 20 percent loss and then buy his car from him a year later when he no longer enjoys it or has moved on to another vehicle. Materialistic trendsetters are usually horrendous bargain shoppers, but they are fun to party with.

The closest I came to topping this was when I landed a gig based on my looks, and not in a cool "Big Al Models" type of way. Time Warner was having a DVD release party for *Scooby-Doo* and promoting the upcoming *Scooby-Doo 2: Monsters Unleashed.* The company needed a Shaggy look-alike, and aside from actually looking like a B-grade Shaggy, the truth is that I have a history of looking like, sounding like, and constantly being mistaken for a big stoner. So it was kind of a match made in heaven: a role I was always destined to play (the role of a Shaggy look-alike, that is). A friend forwarded me the casting notice, I applied, and after submitting a couple of photos of myself and talking to the casting agent on the phone, I got the part.

For the party, I spent three hours dressed as Shaggy and walking a live Great Dane around a packed outdoor event to the live music of the Baha Men (the fine creators of

"Who Let the Dogs Out" and responsible for the main song in the movie, "Scooby D"). It was a pretty sweet deal, as I ran into some celebrities, had free food and drinks, and basically had my picture taken with everyone there. If it weren't for the Baha Men, I may have taken Paddy's crown. We both agreed that the pain and suffering inflicted by their music made the whole evening a push. Paddy and I had tied for the best gig ever. But I apparently impressed the current voice of Scooby-Doo, a radio DJ in Louisiana. He gave me his card and told me he could get me a gig traveling around the world as Shaggy. As he put it, "I have never seen a Shaggy as good as you. You even walk like him!" Upon hearing this backhanded compliment, I laughed and laughed and laughed—and then I cried. That is, until I got my $350 check in the mail for the Shaggy gig, and I finally won my first game of Mailbox Roulette. I ended up declining the touring gig of Shaggy, because I was really looking to make a name for myself as Alan Corey. I believed I had more in me than mimicking an ugly fictional character who was often assumed to be a drug addict.

ALAN COREY 101

Being naturally competitive, I found that turning everything into a game pushed me to being more creative and also allowed me to have more fun with my finances (or lack thereof). It helps to have a friendly rival in these types of games, as the support from that rival can really carry you through the rough times. To an extent, people usually can't control their income—that's what bosses control. Rather than just sit back and accept that fact, you should become a side-gig entrepreneur like me. I aspired to be as good as Paddy, and I came pretty damn close. We all have our strengths and weaknesses, but a balance of saving as much as possible and earning as much as possible is a wonderful combination. Whether it be playing a human guinea pig, bartending one night a week, or mowing your neighbor's lawn for a free dinner, find ways to supplement your day job. It will break up the monotony of your week and give you an edge in your own version of Mailbox Roulette.

> **AGE TWENTY-FOUR AND TWO MONTHS**
>
> **Checking account: $4,100**
> **Savings account: $0**
> **Second, hidden savings account: $?**
> **401(k): $5,300**
> **Mutual fund: $3,300**
> **Roth IRA: $6,000**
> **Equity: $21,500**
> **Total net worth: $40,200**

Chapter 10
Tripped Out

DO *I think your boyfriend's cheating on you? Most likely. It's your wild-card night; you are each supposed to go out on a date and enjoy it, and then tomorrow reassess your relationship. Forget about him, we get free drinks and entertainment all night! Let's take advantage of it. Okay, well, I am going to get as drunk as possible. I want to make this fun. Can you just stop crying for five minutes?*

One of the side gigs I found that paid a decent amount of money was TV shows. This is no secret, but being on TV can earn you big bucks. And any way that I could make money on the side, I was down for. Being twenty-four, I was still trying to figure out my life's true calling, so I started performing at some open-mike comedy shows in the city. (Hard to believe, but I found out that it took talent to be an evil genius or a rock star. Fortunately, open mikes in NYC took anyone.) One night I saw a flyer at one of these open-mike nights looking for comedians to audition for a dating show called *Change of Heart*. I have come to find out that many reality show producers like to cast green wannabe comedians like me. This is probably because of our willingness to do anything, eagerness to be on TV, and potential comedic talents. Or, more likely, our depleted bank accounts.

I auditioned and got cast. The premise was that I would go on a date with a girl who was already in a relationship, and if the date went really well, there was a chance that she'd have a "change of heart" and pick me over her boyfriend the next day. I went on the date, and the girl was pretty awful. All she talked about was her concern that her boyfriend was going to cheat on her. (Umm, *yeah,* that's the point of the show.) But what I thought was cool regardless of the company was a night of free drinks and entertainment, plus a $350 appearance fee. I loved this side gig! (Oh, and, of course, to sweeten the pot, she did have a change of heart and picked me over her loser boyfriend. And I never saw her again.)

A year after my *Change of Heart* appearance, I got offered an audition for *The Restaurant,* a much-hyped reality show documenting the opening of celebrity chef Rocco DiSpirito's newest venture. I got the part, and my "role" on the show was to provide some comedy and to mess up every once in a while, both of which I reluctantly tried to pull off. I didn't mind screwing up an order, but dropping trays and making out with some chick in the meat freezer was where I drew the line (out of respect for Rocco and my significant other, respectively). I respected Rocco as an entrepreneur, and I didn't think it was fair to screw up his dream restaurant for the sake of "good" television. After all, I saw myself in Rocco's shoes one day, and I wouldn't want someone intentionally trying to sabotage my efforts. Due to one of my half-hearted attempts at mucking up the show, I was demoted from a featured waiter role to a food-running background prop. (Sorry peeps, but this is the way "reality" TV shows actually work.)

I actually earned a second living wage as a food runner for six weeks before I quit the show. (After a certain point, I'd had it.) It wasn't a lot of cash, but it *was* a second job for me, earning me some cash that I could apply to my millionaire-by-thirty dream. During this time, I was working nights and weekends at the restaurant, and heading to my tech support job five days a week. Getting paid to be on TV was much better than sitting at home and watching TV earning nothing, which at the time was the alternative. Even if it was exhausting work, it put some extra cash in my wallet. Plus, I got some Diesel jeans and Adidas shoes for free (the work uniform)—and a deeply earned respect for food runners and busboys.

Now, I had learned these benefits of being on TV as a good source of income and other perks when I was in college. Back then, my roommate Jeff and I had a plan that we hoped would produce a free and memorable spring break adventure, rather than going to Florida like we had done every year prior. We decided that we would make up a story, get on a daytime talk show, and let them fly us out to wherever they were filming. It was a far-fetched plan, but we thought it would be amazing if we could pull it off.

At least it would make a good story for the postvacation "What did you do on spring break?" query everyone asks.

We recruited our best girl friends to be part of our charade and called *The Jerry Springer Show* and told them that Jeff and I, best friends and roommates, were dating another pair of best friends and roommates. The kicker: We were all sleeping together—and we wanted to tell the world on *his* show. (Yes, it was a complete lie, but we were desperate for a free trip and would do whatever it took. Yes, it might mean that we would go on the worst show in TV history to save a few bucks, but we were okay with that.)

And the producers loved it. They flew the four of us to Chicago for spring break, all expenses paid: free airfare, free hotels, and free limos. We even got $250 each of "Jerry Bucks," little pieces of paper with Jerry Springer's face on them, redeemable at any hotel gift shop or restaurant. This was the best spring(er) break ever!

We filmed the show, had the requisite onstage fight, stifled our laughter, and then we were on our way back home a few days later. We did it: We got a free spring break trip minus the sunburn, and one that was way cheaper than a drive to Florida. (Only skill it required: calling 1-800-96-JERRY.) Not only that, but we became a hit on campus, and in the end, everyone seemed to agree that we made for pretty good TV. While not the classiest choice, at least *Jerry Springer* was a step up from making our mark in the video *Girls Gone Wild,* which, truthfully, is an option we probably would have sought out if we had ended up in Daytona Beach/Panama City/Boozeville, Florida.

Little did I know, this creative little spring break scheme became my first step down a long and winding path of reality TV gigs—one that earned me some pocket money and a ton of free swag.

Remarkably, during my second year in New York, while I was filming *The Restaurant,* I got picked for *another* reality show due to my insane thriftiness. A friend recommended me for a brand-new makeover show because she knew (1) I was a reality TV whore and (2) I needed a makeover. Backhanded compliments, but I instantly knew it would be fun and would probably mean lots more free stuff. Of course I was down! However, the producers of this new show needed me to pitch a premise of why I needed a makeover. If I could come up with something catchy, then they would book me for the show.

I figured a penny-pinching mooch would be a perfect angle for a new makeover show. I was definitely that, and it showed within every aspect of my life, from home to fashion. I pitched an embellished story line that my new girlfriend's parents were about to meet my parents for the first time at a cocktail party at my house. I didn't tell them that there was actually no need for them to meet (they lived in different states), but I figured it would be a good premise for a makeover event. And so did the producers. Not to mention that my girlfriend at the time was in the "he needs a makeover" corner as well.

This unproven new reality show ended up being *Queer Eye for the Straight Guy,* and, indeed, I did get completely hooked up on the show. First, I should say, the "Fab Five" and I were instant friends, and it was so much fun taping with them for four days, even though the whole show was based on them criticizing me about my cheapskate ways. It was still nonstop fun, and the show did become a hit.

Not to lose track, the reason I do reality shows is that they're fun. And for the goody bag of stuff you get, and I got hooked up on this one. The way it worked was that companies would donate their products to *Queer Eye* to be featured on TV. *Queer Eye* would then turn around and give these goods to their *Queer Eye* victims. I was on season one, which had the lowest budget (and was before all the *Queer Eye* mania), but when all was said and done, I came out on top. I calculated I got about $15,000 worth of free clothes and furniture just for being ridiculed about my stinginess on TV. It was an amazing experience and worth every ounce of embarrassment. I was relearning quickly that if I gave producers good TV, in return I'd get free goods. Yes, it was like being a prostitute, but a very well-dressed prostitute who has kick-ass furniture.

After filming my makeover (and my fourth reality show), I assumed I could never do reality TV again. I had to be blacklisted somewhere at that point. Everyone seemed to recognize me as the stingy fool from *Queer Eye*. Even the *Queer Eye* producers recognized that I was a memorable character. I was so memorable, in fact, I got called back with twenty-four other former *Queer Eye* victims to be on *Queer Eye's Mr. Straight Guy Pageant.* I acted like my usual buffoon self, won second place, and got some more prizes, including Miss Universe's phone number. (She was one of the MCs at the pageant, and she allowed me to take full advantage of our face time together.) I will admit that she didn't call me back. Apparently Miss Universe has standards (after all, she *is* Miss of the *Universe*), but, nevertheless, I like to aim high. And that's a perk I wouldn't have gotten sitting at home watching TV on my couch.

At this point, I knew that reality TV shows (not to mention fans) were sick of me. Fans really started to notice a problem when Bravo and NBC started airing *The Restaurant* and *Queer Eye* back-to-back several times a week: two hours straight of Alan Corey on reality TV! I got hate mail from some viewers who felt deceived. Someone even started a petition to stop running my episodes. There were also online forums calling me all sorts of names. My three favorite quotes from these forums were probably "Alan is a fucking cheap-ass dickwad," "I think he is an asshat. Actually, I'd even go as far as calling him an assclown," and "I don't know if he's a scam or not, but in my book, he's a creepy little famewhore." (Ahh, the beauty of anonymous posting on the Internet.)

So what's a creepy little cheap-ass famewhore to do? Naturally, I moved on to audition for game shows. It seemed a logical transition, and possibly an ample source of money just waiting for me to collect. And, hopefully, not as many eagle-eyed fans. I knew I wouldn't win over everyone. I could barely win over a girl to date me. I'd gladly receive some entertaining barbs in exchange for a fun and profitable side gig like more television appearances.

After a few rejections at the big-time game shows I auditioned for, I finally landed one with a team. Jeff, my New

York roommate Andrew, and I got cast in a new word-association game show called *Chain Reaction* on the Game Show Network. It is a three-on-three team competition. Watching the show, we realized that all the contestants were boring personalities with boring stories (they were friends since high school, all work together, in the same frat, and so on). We knew that if we had a unique angle, we'd get on and get a chance to win some money. So borrowing an idea from my friend's comedy prank Web site, Improv Everywhere, we pretended that the three of us were in a barbershop quartet. Quartet means four, so we informed the producers that the fourth member of the quartet wasn't a fan of the show. They thought that was a valid (and possibly rude) reason, but noticed our hook was distinctive and would make for an interesting show. We got booked, filmed the show a few months later, and wore ridiculous barbershop quartet outfits. Our team completely slaughtered our opponents (don't underestimate the intimidation of candy-striped jackets), and we ended up winning $8,400! Only skill required: renting said jackets. Not bad for some brainstorming and a few hours of filming. Plus, our barbershop quartet hasn't had one online hater. Yet.

ALAN COREY 101

Have a gimmick, a story line, and think outside the box. You never know what people will give you. It could be free trips, clothes, or money, like I earned, to help me penny-pinch a little more. In the beginning, I realized we were helping *Jerry Springer* to put on a good TV show with a story line that they could use. And in return, they were helping us out by giving us a free vacation. It was a win-win for everyone. It took some convincing (and some acting), and it paid off. And no one got hit by a chair! Well, except for Jeff.

For *The Restaurant,* my gimmick was basically to be a distraction and provide some comic relief by bantering with the customers, making mistakes, and committing other blunders. In the audition, I pounded into the heads of the producers my "never been embarrassed" tales and willingness to push the envelope. Although I didn't completely follow through with everything I set out to do, it seemed to work for everyone: I was being entertained and being entertaining enough to make a few appearances throughout season one. Another win-win situation for me and the producers—but not for Rocco, toward whom I felt sympathetic after the first few days.

At this point, I've been on five reality shows and one game show. Why do I do it? Why do I like it? Well, I have no legitimate talents to actually make a living on TV. I just have a willingness to be thoroughly embarrassed on national television, and that opportunity comes often. Plus, it's entertaining to me, and, usually, entertaining to others. And I obviously don't mind being compensated for it, either. I know producers want good TV, and I do my best to give it to them (except if you are asking me to sabotage an entrepreneur I respect). I even turned my gimmick of being on reality shows into a gimmick all its own. I've been paid hundreds of dollars a show to travel around the country to universities and perform my comedic one-man show about my experiences on reality TV. It's called *Creepy Little Fame-whore,* of course.

Through it all, I've learned that a gimmick, a twist, or just a new angle can help you create opportunities. And those opportunities can be turned into other opportunities. This is the cornerstone of many successful people, ideas, and businesses. My idea was just finagling my way onto as many reality TV shows as possible. I currently don't see any more reality TV in my horizon, as people are truly sick of me. But that just shows how successful I was at it. And not one producer ever complained after finding out about my shenanigans, as they were appreciative of what I did for them. It was only those damn viewers on those hate-filled message boards that didn't like me!

AGE TWENTY-FOUR, TWO MONTHS, AND TWO WEEKS
Checking account: $6,200
Savings account: $0
Second, hidden savings account: $?
401(k): $5,300
Mutual fund: $3,300
Roth IRA: $6,000
Equity: $21,500
Total net worth: $42,300

Chapter 11
Basic Instincts

YOUR *car broke down? You want me to give you $20 to get your car fixed. And you'll pay me back $40 tomorrow? Okay. Wow, what broke in your car that costs only $20 to fix? Oh, the belt. Can I see it? Oh, your car's in the shop. The shop is, like, fifteen blocks away. Why are you over here, then? Oh, your aunt lives down the street? What street? I live down the street. Oh, I was thinking I might know your aunt. Why don't you ask your aunt? She lost her job? Sure, sure. Okay, so, yeah, only $20 to fix your car belt. And you'll pay me back $40. Okay, well, I can't help you, because you told me the same story about a month ago. Yeah, I'd try a new shop.*

I like easy money. As someone who is naturally attracted to any deal, contest, or opportunity, I've run across my fair share of scams and illegal propositions. As many people know, anything that requires money up front is a scam. And often scams do have a "too good to be true" vibe that makes them so hard to resist. I was doing okay with my millionaire goal, up to roughly $42,300, and I was still itching to get much more. Any little bit would help. For everyone, it's tempting to try to take the fast track to riches when it's offered to you, like all those Nigerian lottery scams and pyramid schemes. I had those opportunities and more, but I just had to remind myself that making money, especially a lot of money, takes a lot of hard work. So if anything was pitched to me with an "easy breezy" path to riches, then I had to trust my gut instinct that it was probably a scam.

Recently, my friend Allison was walking down the street and was stopped by a modeling recruiter. She told her that she looked beautiful, passed her a business card, and invited her to come in to the office the next day for an evaluation. Allison was excited, of course, and she couldn't wait to go. Allison's attractive, so it wasn't completely out of the realm of possibility that something like this might happen. (Improbable, sure, but not impossible.)

But Allison didn't want to go by herself, and she begged me to go. I was completely hungover, but I finally agreed, as the opportunity to see several models in one room seemed worthy of the effort. I had slept in my clothes from the night before (it was Halloween, after all, and I was still wearing part of my disco costume of a powder blue leisure suit). Being hungover, thus slow moving, I didn't have time to change. Forty-five minutes later, I met her out front of the modeling agency looking like a dead 1970s John Travolta. I explained that I made no effort to look good in order to make her look more attractive. I don't think she bought it, but she was happy I was there nevertheless.

The place was the slickest place I've ever seen. There were flat-screen TVs in every room showing runway models, magazine covers framed along the wall, and the loudest music pulsing through a place of business that I have ever heard. Once inside, Allison was given a whole bunch of forms to fill out. As I sat waiting on the bench in the lobby, a nicely dressed man from the agency approached me and offered me the same forms, explaining that I had "an interesting look," and that as long as I was there, I might as well get an evaluation as well. I had nothing else to do, so I filled them out. And I'm not one to ever turn down a chance to be in the spotlight, hungover or not. After about thirty minutes, the waiting room became filled with attractive men and women—not necessarily *model* attractive, but people who were a little above average in the looks department. But by comparison, the people that worked at the agency were far better looking than anyone in this cattle call I was now a part of. Then a hot agency representative called us in one by one for an evaluation. This place seemed legit, or at least it would be exciting to be associated with such a cool and trendy atmosphere.

I went first. The spiel they gave me was that they were a modeling agency with connections to all the big casting agents, magazines, and producers. They followed this with a hurricane of compliments, telling me how great and unique I looked, and that we could make a lot of money together. For anyone who wanted to hear such a thing, it was fairly intoxicating stuff: These people were pretty convincing.

They explained to me that all I needed to get started was a portfolio of photos to show to agents, and then they would get started casting me. Of course, they couldn't guarantee me they would get me any roles or gigs, but they couldn't try until I had a book to show people.

Extreme Cheapskate Strategy

Many gyms and health clubs offer you a free trial week. Spend time to research them and take advantage of this offer. When you travel out of state, say you are new in town and would like to try out the gym; it's definitely going to be better than any hotel workout facilities. I kept this up for three months once, finally stopping after I was driving forty-five minutes to go work out each day in a different town. You can choose your own limits (mine being the city limits).

Oh, but the book had to be done by a professional photographer, and even though I didn't know any professional photographers, I was in luck, because they *happened* to have some in-house photographers that they could recommend. And, bonus: The fee for their guy would be about $500 cheaper than if I went anywhere else—but it was ultimately my choice, of course. So I could spend $2,000 using my own photographer or use theirs for $1,500.

For me, and for many other people, probably, the scam was easy to spot, but I'm sure for those who were desperate or seduced by the idea of fame, it was hard to say no. They really tried to make it seem like you were just $1,500 away from stardom. But like anything that requires payment up front, they were taking people for a ride.

After they were done with me, Allison got called. She went in and came out, and, of course, got the exact same routine I did. Everyone in the room ended up being told the same thing. Some "evaluation"—it turned out that everyone passed! None of us was model material, but of course we all wanted to be. Who wouldn't? The sham modeling agency was just preying on people's insecurities and dreams, and it herded in a whole new group of people every single day. If one person bit, that was $1,500 in the scam artists' pockets, and then they'd put no real effort into casting the person. If the person complained that he or she wasn't getting cast, the agency would tell him or her to get new photos—maybe with a different look this time, and to use its photographer again. But now, since the person was a "client," the fee was only $1,200. And the cycle would never stop.

I ran across another "deal" when I was in a Polish neighborhood in Brooklyn. I was at a bar one night and became friendly with a bunch of guys who had had a little too much to drink. They were telling me about how much trouble they were having getting green cards to stay in the United States. The thing was, they weren't trying to do it the legal way: They'd all paid American girls to pretend to marry them. If they kept the marriage front going for a certain number of years, they could get a divorce and still remain in the United States. After some digging, I found out these guys didn't live with the women, barely knew the women, and, well, that was the crux of their problem.

Each fake couple would get interviewed by the United States Citizenship and Immigration Services every year, and—surprise—they all kept screwing up the interviews. The spouses wouldn't know each other's birthdays, or what their dog's name was, or some other detail that people who are *actually* married tend to have no problems recalling. It all seemed very nerve racking, not to mention completely illegal. And then they pitched the scam to me.

They were planning on bringing their sister over to the States and wanted to know if I would be willing to "marry" her. Sure, I would have to go through the USCIS interviews every couple of years, but after three years, they would pay me $15,000. Now, I like the sound of $15,000, but the thought of following through with something like that scared me to death. Luckily, this was all pitched to me over my first beer, so I didn't make an intoxicated decision I later regretted. I got out of there pretty quickly with a solid no. And rather than falling for easy money, whether it was a scam or not, I held on to the money I had already earned the hard and legit way. The fast track doesn't exist in unearned riches.

ALAN COREY 101

If it's too good to be true, then it probably is. When things are tight financially or you're feeling like you're not reaching your goal fast enough, it's tempting to chase a golden carrot being dangled in front of you. But the fact is, there is no quick and easy way to get rich. If you think there is, you will just throw away your hard-earned money and dig a deeper financial hole for yourself. My feeling is that if I don't have to work hard for the money, the money probably isn't there.

Unless you're paying for school or a class that will help you reach your goal, you shouldn't pay up front for anything. You can't pay someone money to do something that you need to do for yourself; for example, Allison couldn't *buy* herself a modeling or acting career, but if she really wanted to be a model, she could have done some research and found out exactly how someone breaks into the business. And she probably could have gotten a lot of answers for less than $1,500, if not for free.

You're vulnerable to scams only if you don't know what you want, don't have a plan, and don't know how other people who achieved goals similar to yours succeeded. Once you know what you want, learn everything you can about the topic, industry, and so forth, and use that knowledge to plot out the steps to get you there. If you do that, no one will be able to distract you by offering the "easy way" out, because you'll be focused and already know what you need to do to get you where you want to be.

The millions of dollars are out there. You just have to get them the hard way, by working hard and being smart. Not by being foolish. People lose millions falling for various pie-in-the-sky scams. Luckily, I didn't have to learn the lesson the hard way. My instincts knew what was best.

AGE TWENTY-FOUR AND THREE MONTHS

Checking account: $6,900

Savings account: $0

Second, hidden savings account: $?

401(k): $5,300

Mutual fund: $3,300

Roth IRA: $6,000

Equity: $21,500

Total net worth: $43,000

PART III

Brokering and Budgeting

Chapter 12
Treasure Hunt

THIS *bathroom is disgusting. It's the only thing keeping the apartment from being considered above average. If I make over the bathroom, I'll have more equity in the place because it will be worth more. If I ever move out, I can rent it out for more. Man, what is happening to me? I bet this is what adults think like all the time: "Let's do bathroom makeovers!" Didn't I just throw a massive beer bash? What's happened to me? Jesus H. Wheelchair, I'm getting so old!*

Eleven months into property owning, I was spending a lot of time thinking about bathroom makeovers. It was slightly unsettling, like the feeling of finding yourself caring about an *American Idol* finalist. But I had saved enough money to get one, so I decided to go ahead and do it. I got estimates from several **contractors and handymen** and went with the second-cheapest guy, who was also the one who promised the work would be completed the earliest. I even had him sign an agreement that if the job wasn't done by the date we agreed on, he'd take $300 off the bill, which actually brought his price down to the lowest bid I got.

I did a complete **gut renovation** of the bathroom: new shower, new tile, new sink, new toilet, and new overhead lights. The total price was $6,000.

Now, when you renovate your home, and you do it right, you raise the value of the property close to equal, or sometimes even more than, the money you spent to fix it up. Studies show that bathroom and kitchen renovations are the most effective in helping owners recoup expenses and increase the value of their home. Buyers (and renters) care about these two areas the most when looking at properties. It probably has something to do with our society's obsession with food and potty humor. My bathroom was in such bad shape, I figured that if I spent $6,000 to renovate it by buying tile, a toilet, and a sink at discount prices, hired a low-priced quality contractor, and painted it myself, I could end up adding $10,000 in value to my apartment. It seemed like another win-win situation to me. I got it done quickly and for the cheapest price. (The job was completed a day late, so I got $300 knocked off the price, as agreed.) And it looked great; the apartment was now complete. Now I just had to find a way to buy another one.

Around the time of the bathroom makeover, my two-year anniversary of extreme saving was approaching, and I was getting ready to check my finances once again. It was two and a half years since I had moved to New York City. My checking account balance was low after paying for the bathroom makeover, but I reminded myself that my equity had gone up because of the money I had spent. Additionally, my equity had also increased because, as I had hoped, the New York real-estate market was on the rise.

This is how it works: The value of real estate is based on **comparables.** In my situation, all of the apartments similar to mine in my building and on my block were selling for more money than they had been a year before. If I had decided to sell my apartment, I would have gotten more money than I had paid in 2002, because the comparables in the neighborhood were going up. If I didn't sell, the difference between what I paid and what I could get would be reflected in my equity, since my apartment was worth more than it was when I bought it.

I had a real-estate agent come by post–bathroom renovation, and as I had planned, he told me that he could sell the place for $130,000. Fantastic. When I looked at my balances overall, I could see that the value of my stocks had decreased a little bit over the past year, but the value of my real estate had increased greatly. By owning property, I was in a position to benefit in both markets, which meant that I had a balanced portfolio. In other words, I didn't have all of my eggs in one basket. I could tolerate some loss in one area and was able to benefit from the gains in another, which in my case was real estate.

You'll notice in my tally at the end of this chapter that the principal on my mortgage is now $600 lower, as I had been paying it off (along with interest) throughout the year.

As a result, I had added to my overall equity since equity = value − what you owe. I owed less, so I was worth more.

In just over one year, I had added $24,500 to my overall financial picture by adding to my mutual fund, Roth IRA, and equity. I had benefited from a positive real-estate upswing and wasn't too hurt by a slow stock market. And I had an undisclosed amount still in my hidden savings account.

So I had $24,500 more, but I still wanted to buy more real estate. I had decided that my secondary goal, after being a millionaire by thirty, was to purchase one property a year. I would keep buying places and renting them out, so I would have someone else paying my mortgage on each property. A fine idea, but with $900 in my checking account, I knew I didn't have enough money for a down payment on anything that didn't have a cardboard roof. But I wasn't about to give up on my goal. I just needed to figure out another way to make it work. I decided to talk to a professional, just to see if there was any possibility I could buy another property.

I scheduled an appointment with a **mortgage broker,** which is someone who applies for mortgages at several different banks on your behalf and then comes back to you with the best offer.

Tip: If you're shopping online, *never, ever* buy anything without searching to see if there's an online coupon that can save you some money. Just Google "online coupon" and the product name. There are sites on the Web devoted exclusively to keeping track of who's offering what discount for how long. Sometimes you can score free shipping, sometimes 20 percent off. If you don't use them, you're just throwing away money.

Honestly, I expected the meeting to be pretty quick, one that started with him laughing in my face and ended with him telling me to come back when I had some money. But that wasn't what happened. I did have money in the form of net worth, and that's something. If I added up my 401(k), Roth IRA, equity, and checking and savings accounts, I had money. It was my hands-off money, I didn't want to spend it, but I had access to it. And I hoped that would get me somewhere.

He sat me down and let me know all of my options. (I really didn't think I *had* any options.) He explained that it was possible for me to do a *zero-down* deal (which is exactly what it sounds like: putting no money down), but that would mean I'd have high monthly payments. If I did want to go with zero down, he could get me a loan for $150,000 based on the value of all my assets (stocks, equity, and bank accounts).

I was pumped—I could get a place after all! But the mortgage broker kept talking, so I kept listening. He asked me if I had any interest in a **multifamily home.**

I wasn't sure what that entailed, but it sounded expensive. He explained that was a fancy way of saying "a building with more than one unit," and that I could live in one apartment and rent out the others. And then he said this: If I were interested in purchasing a multifamily home, he would be able to approve me for a $500,000 loan. *I freaked out.* A half million dollars! I thought he was smoking crack. He just said he would give me a half million dollars! I thought maybe *I* had just smoked crack. What the hell was going on? I caught my breath after about five minutes, and then I made him explain how the Fred Savage this was possible.

He told me that if I bought a multifamily home, the property's rental units would generate income that could be used to pay off my mortgage. Those sources of income would make the investment less risky, so banks would be more willing to provide me with a large loan to finance the purchase.

We both knew there was no way I would be able to afford the $4,000 monthly payments that came with a $500,000 no-money-down loan. But if I could find a multifamily house that I could rent out for a combined $4,000 a month, then a bank would approve the loan. The tricky part, of course, was that I had to find a place under $500,000 with a rental income of $4,000. I didn't know what lay ahead, but it was definitely worth a try. It was just so crazy, it just might work. I had to start this treasure hunt ASAP; I wanted this $500,000 loan before this mortgage dude changed his mind, like my mom did with her matched-savings plan!

ALAN COREY 101

Having subgoals that support your overall big goal is also crucial to achieving anything. If you have only one big, lofty goal floating off in the future, it's easy to feel over-whelmed, discouraged, and at a loss as to how you're going to get there. Subgoals provide the road map that tells you how. Subgoals help you know where you're going and pro-vide an achievable goal to focus on. Every time you accom-plish one of your minigoals, you know you're one step closer to the big goal, and you also reap the benefit of in-creased confidence, which will only spur you to get crack-ing on the next step in your plan.

I know this works, because it's what happened to me. My subgoal of being a millionaire by thirty was to buy real estate every single year, and my commitment to that helped introduce me to the idea of owning multifamily homes—something I probably never would have thought of if I hadn't focused on figuring out how to buy another prop-erty. I found that each time I accomplished one of my sub-goals, I felt that much closer to my ultimate goal of being a millionaire by thirty. It was something that could be easily measured, and each time I took that next step, the progress from that would keep me motivated to keep on going. Figure out whatever you want to do; then decide on the steps you need to accomplish that goal. And then: Get going!

AGE TWENTY-FOUR AND FIVE MONTHS
Checking account: $900
Savings account: $0
Second, hidden savings account: $?
401(k): $6,400
Mutual fund: $4,200
Roth IRA: $6,000
Equity: $40,000
Total net worth: $57,500

Chapter 13
Friends Who
Take Interest

A half million dollars! I can have a $500,000 shopping spree! Jesus H. Moneybags! I need to find a place, and fast. I'm only twenty-four years old; this is ridiculous. Okay, calm down. Walk around this open house. Act like you know what you are doing. Be cool. Let the agent think you might buy. Ask a lot of questions. Listen to what other people are asking. Get a flyer. Breathe. Breathe. Count to ten: one, two, three—a half million dollars!

I went to work immediately. I hunted all over and went to as many multifamily open houses as possible. Sometimes the agents had the rent roll (the income it produced) of the property, sometimes not. When they didn't, I would go check out rentals in the building's neighborhood, to get an idea of what the going rates were. Many of the properties I saw for sale were listed at over $500,000 or had a rental income of less than $4,000. Finding a building was turning out to be harder than finding a girl who didn't think I was a cheapskate, but I couldn't give up. My house had to be out there somewhere.

One day, as I was exploring my neighborhood and the surrounding areas, I happened upon an open house. There had been a fire in the two-family house a few years before, and the owner had renovated it with the cheapest and ugliest stuff possible. It had been sitting empty for two years. It wasn't pretty, but it was really big, and it even had a backyard, which is highly prized in New York City. But the best part was that it was listed for $450,000; I just had to figure out the building's rental income.

One unit in the house was a three-bedroom. After doing some research, I found out that another ugly three-bedroom in the same neighborhood was going for $1,500 a month. The second unit was also a three-bedroom, but it had an office, too, and I guessed that office had to be worth around $500. That meant the total rental income of the property was $3,500. It wasn't the $4,000 I needed, but the building didn't cost $500,000, either. I had to go back to the mortgage broker to see if this could work.

He punched some numbers into his computer and came back with bad news. **Interest rates** had changed a bit since the last time we talked, and now I would need to earn $4,000 a month in rent to get a $450,000 loan with nothing down. So I dug deeper and asked him if there was *any* way the deal could be done. He told me that if I came up with a 10 percent down payment, I could get the monthly amount I would need to make from renting to tenants down to a target number of $3,500.

At first, I didn't think that would be possible; I didn't *have* $45,000 to fork over. But it seemed like that was the only way it was going to happen. I had to get creative and find a way to make the deal work.

I went back to my apartment and brainstormed. I figured that my only hope was to try to lowball again, so I called up the agent and offered $400,000. No dice: She hinted that she had an offer much closer to the asking price. I had to get this place; nothing else I had seen had come this close to having the numbers work out for me. How could I come up with a $45,000 down payment?

It would take me forever to save that amount. I didn't want to cash out my 401(k), mutual funds, and Roth IRA. Those options all came with hefty penalties and I wanted to keep those invested in stocks for the long term. The only option seemed to be to flat-out borrow the money. I didn't know any huge benefactor with a lot of cash to throw around, but I *did* know a few people with a little bit of money. I decided it was worth a try, and I went to the people who trusted me the most: my parents.

I first pitched the deal to my mother (my extremely cheap mother), and she was, of course, nervous. She's always nervous with risking money, and she's never liked parting with any of it, no matter how little. She finally agreed to give me $10,000, but I had to pay her back in full in two years. On top of that, I would have to pay back the loan with an additional 10 percent interest. That was probably more than a bank would charge me, but then again, with my financial situation, a bank probably wasn't going to give me $10,000 to begin with. I figured that in a worst-case scenario, I could sell my apartment and pay her back.

Next I went to my dad. He said the same thing he always says to me: "What does your mother think about this?" I told him that Mom gave me $10,000 at 10 percent interest. My dad said he would do the same thing. I also promised him I would sell my apartment to get the money to pay him back if necessary.

I now had $20,000 in my hands, which was great, but I still needed $25,000 more. I went to two of my best friends, Fat Matt and Tall Phil. It was weird asking my friends for a chunk of money, but I told them about the deal I struck with my parents and offered it to them too: paid back in full in two years, plus 10 percent interest. I told them I would cash out my 401(k) and Roth IRA and pay them back if necessary. I was young enough that if it didn't work out, and I did have to drain my retirement fund—which, really, you should avoid at all costs—I could start my 401(k) investing plan all over again. It wasn't the best disaster plan, it was my worst-case-scenario disaster plan, but I had decided that I needed to take a big risk. After some sleepless nights, they agreed to help me out. They both lent me $10,000. Friends are nice; rich friends who will put up ten grand each are *really nice!* (Thanks, Fat Matt and Tall Phil!)

Extreme Cheapskate Strategy

Buy one pair of multipurpose shoes a year. Don't buy any others. If shoes make or break you with any business deal, date, or interview, believe me, unless it's a girl with a foot fetish, it isn't the shoes.

And to prove that sometimes day jobs aren't all that bad, I found a way to convince my boss to give me a full year-end bonus and a slight raise. Picking up on my first year-end review, I reused my strategy that worked before. Since day one of employment, I saved every thank-you e-mail any customer sent me after I answered his or her question on the computer hotline. I saved anything containing praise about the speed of my work, the quality of my work, and more. And if I had a good rapport with the customer, I'd ask him or her to send an e-mail to my boss saying that same thing, and to copy me on the e-mail. So during my year-end bonus review, I presented a stack of printed e-mails showing what great work I was doing. It's hard to say no to documented proof, no matter how much of a slacker I really was around the office. And believe me, I had played over three thousand games of Tetris, so I was the king of slackers. My reward? A $5,000 bonus once again, giving me the last of the money I needed. I had enough for a down payment!

I had two years to figure out how to pay back my friends and parents, but I knew that my expenses weren't going to go up, and I planned to continue saving like crazy. With the raise, I had a little more money coming in each month now, and I still continued working odd side gigs. I thought about even getting a legitimate second job if necessary, but only if I had trouble finding some renters. I was above water for the time being, but I was mentally preparing myself in case I hit some financial rough patches.

I called back the agent and offered the asking price of $450,000 with 10 percent down. I got a call back that same day, and the owners accepted my offer. The house was mine!

Just six weeks later, I was closing on the house. I showed up with my checkbook and a smile. The agent even told me she was glad that I had gotten the place, saying she thought I would make the best use of it. After about two hours of signing papers and giving handshakes, I was a twenty-four-year-old who owned two properties. My portfolio had changed drastically once again.

> **Tip:** Never invest your money in something you don't completely understand. You've worked hard for your money, so work hard at investing your money.

That feeling was awesome, but now things were really tight financially. Drastic times called for drastic measures: I put a temporary stop to my monthly $200 automatic mutual fund investment. I had to focus on keeping up with my mortgage payments, paying back my friends and family, and finally building up an **emergency fund,** as I should have been doing all along (in case things really went sour).

In my head, I had my stocks as my emergency fund, although that was technically cheating. Plus, I had just promised them to my friends as collateral if I defaulted on my loan, so things were tight, for sure. Maintaining my lifestyle of extreme saving was now more important than ever, especially because I now had other people's money on the line. And though they were not the types to break kneecaps, the shame and guilt would have been far worse. I had to make it work. I had no choice. I just had to remain super-optimistic if I encountered any hiccups along the way.

ALAN COREY 101

When you see an opportunity, one that is key to your financial picture, don't give up on it. Find a way to make it work, but at the same time formulate an escape plan. That's not being defeatist, it's just being prepared. I saw the house as a big step toward being a millionaire by thirty, and I was determined to get it. But I also knew that if it didn't work out, I could cover my debts. I also had a credit card to put expenses on if I got into real trouble, although I definitely knew to avoid that route if at all possible. That was worst-worst-worst-case scenario.

If you don't get what you want at first, try another tactic, and if that doesn't work, think of another strategy. I found out all of my options from a mortgage broker, and then put in a low bid on the house. When that didn't work, I went to my family and friends, but I wasn't asking them to *give* me money. It's never a crime to ask for help. The key is figuring out how the people who can help you can benefit from doing so—then you're helping *each other.*

My favorite part of having a day job was the year-end review. This is usually hated by both boss and subordinate. I looked at it as my one chance to get a bonus and a raise. So thinking ahead a full year, I collected everything to help me with my case. It worked the first year, so I made sure it would work again. Plus, I knew I had a difficult case to present. My mind was always on personal projects rather than the company's needs. (If not Tetris, then it was real estate, side gigs, and fantasy football.) Yes, I was reliable and professional, but I never went above and beyond my responsibilities in the office. I had other things to deal with (like winning fantasy football). However, I knew I needed that money, and I found a way to get that bonus. This strategy worked for me time and time again.

I avoided tapping into my hidden savings account—that was now for emergency purposes only. It was using other people's money that helped me take a major step toward being a millionaire. If I hadn't enlisted their help and taken that risk, I would probably be in a very different financial position than I am now.

AGE TWENTY-FOUR AND SIX MONTHS

Checking account: $500

Savings account: $0

Second, hidden savings account: $?

401(k): $9,000

Mutual fund: $5,150

Roth IRA: $6,000

Equity on apartment: $40,000

Equity on house: $0 ($450,000 value – $45,000 debt to friends/family – $405,000 mortgage)

Total net worth: $60,650

Chapter 14
Rooms with a Few

THAT'S *what the ad says. Yes, you'll have six roommates. Yes, some of them are strangers to me. It's going well, been doing it for several months now. There are three bathrooms, so you don't have to worry about waiting in line to use the toilet. That seems to be everyone's concern. Also, there are two kitchens. Yes, strange situation. It used to be two units, now it's one. It's hard to explain. If you're interested, I would just suggest you come over and see it. The place is huge, I think you'll like it. You might make some friends. And it's priced well too!*

I had accomplished another goal: I owned more real estate—a multifamily, no less!—and I was now a landlord, which meant that other people were going to pay my mortgage for me. It was exciting, mainly because I had a new title with the word *lord* in it. But slightly terrifying, because I was basically broke and owed all kinds of money—to the bank, to my family, and to friends. I had to figure out a way to maximize the income from my two properties.

The going rate for a nice three-bedroom in the area was about $1,750, so getting $3,500 from my two-family was absolutely doable. After all, one apartment had an office, and one unit had access to the backyard. But I really wanted, and needed, to make more money off the house.

So I came up with the following plan: I'd convert the two-family into a one-family, and rent out the rooms at different rates according to their size. (The "renovation" process amounted to taking a door off its hinges.) So, basically, rather than having two units with three bedrooms each, I had one big house consisting of six individual one-bedrooms for rent. My friends had said they would be willing to pay at least $700 to live in the smallest bedroom in the house, so renting a medium-sized room for $725 seemed reasonable. After converting the house into a one-family structure, I also decided to rent out the office as a bedroom too, now making it seven one-bedroom places to rent with two shared kitchens and living rooms. Lastly, I decided that I too would move in to the house and move out of my $1,100-a-month apartment. The reason? I found a friend who would rent it from me for $1,200, scoring me an extra $100 a month of income in the process.

I drafted some rates for the individual rooms in the house, and this is how it broke down:

One small room, $650
Four medium-sized rooms, $725 each
One master bedroom, $0 (mine)
One office with no windows, $600
Total monthly rent: $4,150

Total rent: $4,150—$650 more than if I had kept the building a two-family! This was definitely the smartest plan financially, and I was excited about putting together a fun and livable rooming-house situation. To help me do that, I intentionally kept the rent for each room low so that I could fill the spots fast and have a choice of roommates, rather than being forced to accept just anyone who applied. I envisioned myself living with good friends and hot models, not Hells Angels and meth heads. My strategy worked. After I sent out some e-mails and posted some ads online, I had more than a handful of potential roommates to choose from. (Although no hot models ever applied.)

I realized that I really didn't know what I was doing and had to educate myself fast. I bought a few books on how to be a landlord, interrogated my real-estate attorney (real-estate attorneys are required when purchasing real estate in New York, so I knew a couple), and went back to doing some online research. I came away with blank lease forms, a basic knowledge of the renting process, and some much-needed confidence.

I quickly filled the rooms with a combination of friends and people I had just met who I thought would be a good fit. I was creating the kind of college lifestyle in the world of adults that I had been shooting for. It turned out to be sort of like college, a bit like MTV's *The Real World,* and slightly insane. We were, after all, seven people (some of them strangers) living together and "getting real" in one big Brooklyn house. Maybe too real. It became *The Real World: Brooklyn.* Which, if you ask me, is better than getting stuck with *The Surreal Life.* But it did come with all the same drama.

One determined roommate had insomnia and kept switching rooms with everyone in the house to try to see if that would help alleviate his disorder. It never did. As often happens in living situations like this, two frisky roommates hooked up with each other on and off. Another got pistol-whipped and robbed walking home late one night; he moved out the next day.

Two strong-willed/weak-brained tenants started a war over who bought and used the most toilet paper. The war ended after a span of three months when my basement got flooded with sewage. As the plumber explained, "A ridiculous amount of paper towels was in the pipes." (That made sense: Paper towels were the backup choice during the toilet paper feud.)

One sexually curious renter was sleeping with a married couple down the street, and one girl who was socially conscious would invite the local homeless population over to feed them. The musically inclined roommate had weekly midnight band practice in the attached house next door, which conveniently took place in the room adjacent to mine. And, no, his group never got a record deal.

All of this made for an interesting dynamic, to say the least, and I learned to refine my roommate selection process by favoring word of mouth and referrals from other friends over complete strangers needing a place to live.

The saving grace was that we were living in a two-family house, which meant we all, crazy or not, had plenty of room. We had two kitchens, two living rooms, and three full bathrooms. It definitely wasn't cramped, and everyone had free reign of everything.

There were other headaches too. A few months after moving in, my roof had to be retarred because rainwater was about to make my ceiling give way; it set me back a painful $6,000. I knew it was in need of repair; however, I hadn't done my homework up front to find out exactly how much it would cost. A home inspector I hired told me the roof would last me one more year, maybe two. He was wrong.

> **Tip:** Do yourself a huge favor and don't shop with your credit card; it'll keep you from spending money you don't have.

The pipes in a neighbor's attached house froze, and his house wasn't flooded, but mine was. He promised to pay me for all the damages; it's been three years, and I'm still waiting for his $2,000 check. I think it will come the same day my tenant's band gets a Grammy.

I also had to deal with the challenges of living with friends who were also my tenants. They wanted a break on rent, thought they didn't have to pay on time, or wanted to renegotiate a lease two weeks after one had been signed. As much as I wanted a casual living environment, I still had to explain that living in the house was a business relationship, since money was involved, and that was hard.

Nevertheless, things were going well, if not a bit mad-cap. The only real snag was the $600 windowless office, which was turning out to be harder to rent than I thought. When we all moved in, I'd found someone to take the office for three months, but in no time at all, his lease was up, and he was moving out.

I couldn't get anyone to bite on taking over his spot, so I decided that the only thing I could do was live there my-self. I figured I could take the shit and rent the gold: the master bedroom I had been using. I moved into the office and went to work on renting out the master bedroom for $800 a month, which took no time at all. My only regret was that I hadn't come up with that idea in the beginning! (Shocking, seeing as how I never flinch at living below my means.)

With this adjustment, my total monthly rent roll had improved yet again:

> **One small room, $650**
> **Four medium-sized rooms, $725 each**
> **One master bedroom, $800**
> **One office with no windows, $0 (mine)**
> **One apartment, $1,200**
> **Total monthly rent: $5,550**

My monthly property expenses were the following:

> **House mortgage, $3,500**
> **Apartment mortgage, $700**
> **Apartment maintenance fees, $400**
> **Total monthly expenses: $4,600**
> **Total monthly profit from real estate: $950**

In short, I was getting paid $950 a month for living in my own house! I had no living expenses besides food and entertainment, and that figure never broke more than $300 a month. Insurance, utilities, taxes, and repairs would take a cut of my monthly profit, but overall I was still coming out way on top for sleeping in my own house and collecting rent checks each month.

Even with this development, I was still working my day job, still putting 15 percent of my paycheck toward my 401(k), and still making a deposit into my Roth IRA. (I had cut back on my mutual fund contribution only temporarily.) Plus, I was still earning savings bonds from my credit card, still working the occasional side gig here and there, and still eating way too much ramen. All my penny-pinching, deal making, and hard work were paying off more than I ever anticipated! I was making a decent income with no viable skills, after all. Given all of this, I estimated that I would probably be able to pay off my friends and family within two years as I had promised, without cashing in my collateral. My income was higher than all my expenses, thanks to my rooming-house situation, and my day job was no longer an economic necessity, as I still had income from side gigs and was still saving as much as possible. Things were actually working out, and even though I had planned it, I couldn't quite believe it. I imagine it would be like what a pot farmer feels when watching crops grow. Sure, he'd planted all the seeds, but look at all that free ganja!

ALAN COREY 101

Once again, I used my go-to strategy of being resourceful and creative. This is the best way to handle any tightly run endeavor. I got more income from my properties by mishmashing tenants together, rather than being conventional and renting out two units. It was more work and more headaches, but it was also more income.

It was also my first stint as a landlord. Landlording wasn't something I had ever thought of doing, but I knew that didn't mean I couldn't do it. I just hadn't done it *before.* I had to educate myself and build up my confidence. It wasn't rocket science, judging by the look of my first (and last) landlord, not even close. I just read as much as I could on landlord-tenant situations, so that I was as prepared as I could be. And still things happened that I hadn't anticipated.

You can never be prepared for everything, and in unique situations like the roof caving in, the basement flooding, and my roommates moving out with only twenty-four hours' notice, I just had to roll with the punches. I did have thoughts of *What the hell did I get myself into?* several times during my first year of landlording, but I was committed to this project, and I had to make it work. If I got unnerved and too frantic, I couldn't dwell on it—that would only make the rough patches rougher. I just had to keep on truckin'.

Another milestone I reached was finally having no living expenses. This was a necessary (and huge) step to getting me where I wanted to be: a millionaire by the age of thirty. I had reduced my cost of living to such a minuscule amount, it didn't take much rental income to cover it. I was able to achieve this goal by renting the best rooms in my house and accepting to live in the worst room. I didn't need a master bedroom, I needed a couple extra hundred dollars a month. I would get the master bedroom someday, but I didn't need it then. I was getting paid to live in an office. That made me happier than any master bedroom could.

Lastly, I still have to thank the mortgage broker for explaining the benefits of having a multifamily house. I just took it one step further and created even more units by renting out the bedrooms separately. I was young, it didn't matter. I brought the dorm life back to NYC, and it was a helluva lot of fun, not to mention a helluva lot of income. And that was an important lesson to learn: Even with all the *Real World* drama, making money can be fun as shit.

AGE TWENTY-FOUR AND SEVEN MONTHS

Checking account: $500

Savings account: $0

Second, hidden savings account: $?

401(k): $10,000

Mutual fund: $5,150

Roth IRA: $6,000

Equity on apartment: $40,000

Equity on house: $0 ($450,000 value – $45,000 debt to friends/family – $405,000 mortgage)

Total net worth: $61,650

Chapter 15
Pressing Matters

WAIT, *is my life miserable, or is it awesome? I can't tell. I scrape by, work hard, and what is the reward? There are so many things I'd rather be doing, and so many things I would like to have, and I'm definitely getting a little burned out on this extreme savings program. On the other hand, I've never been happier. I feel like I'm making progress; hell,* I know *I'm making progress. I have saved enough to buy a house, or at least an apartment. That's a huge accomplishment right there. But is this millionaire goal worth all this work? Well, I've been a little insane, yes, but I truly am enjoying the madness of it all. It's a ridiculous feeling, I know I'm doing more than enough on my savings, but it's so much fun pushing myself to new limits each day. Okay, my life isn't miserable, it's awesome. I've stuck with it for three years, and if I just ride it out to my thirties, I'll be one really rich dude, and then I can quit my day job, travel, and "live it up." When I'm a millionaire, I will live that life I've dreamed about. The one in the rap videos, but without having to return the Rolls at the end of the shoot.*

On the whole, I was doing all right. Amazingly, I was still able to score an occasional girlfriend, even though I was an extreme cheapskate. (A boyfriend with the rule of staying in one night a weekend to toil on PlayStation is not impressive to most women.) Things were tough financially, but I still found ways to enjoy myself, even on a self-imposed tight budget. The million-dollar light was at the end of the tunnel, but I was definitely still in the tunnel. I'd been living a restricted lifestyle for a couple of years, denying myself food delivery in any form and limiting my access to most of my money, and I decided that I wanted to finally reward myself for all my hard work. But I wasn't ready to abandon my plan to be a millionaire or be sidetracked from that goal. I needed to reward myself while also sticking to my goal and savings plan.

My solution was the Billfold Blowout™. Every Sunday morning I'd walk to my bank's ATM—past all the other ATMs that charged me $1.50 per transaction—and withdraw $100. I was sick of accounting for every penny. I wanted to have a little leeway, and this would still keep me on track. The rules were simple: I could spend only $100 a week. I was not allowed to go back to the ATM or use my credit card until the following Sunday. This one ATM trip became my church outing, and I paid my respects to the fee-free machine once a week.

I *also* made it a rule that I had to spend all $100 by the following Sunday. If it was Saturday night, and I had $2, I'd go get some ramen noodles and play some Madden NFL

Football. If I had $60, I would go out, watch a movie on opening night, catch a cab to meet my friends, and then drink myself broke. It was perfect. I was on a budget, but for once it didn't feel like it. My new strategy didn't require always taking the cheapest option, always hunting for a grocery store treasure, or analyzing every single purchase for an hour. It was the best budget system ever. Plus, I got to reward myself greatly on Saturdays if I had any leftover money. If I didn't, it was back to the good ol' days of counting pennies to see what I would eat for dinner. (It was always ramen. I definitely should get my sodium levels checked.)

The truth is that the best weekend night I ever had on my Billfold Blowout plan was the result of the most creative six days I had prior to it, and it barely cost me a cent. My all-time favorite band, OutKast, was playing Madison Square Garden one Saturday night, and, clearly, I couldn't afford to go. I'd been a fan of OutKast's since they were just a local Atlanta rap duo with a misspelled name, and now they were Grammy Award winners on a world tour. I was determined to be there. Obviously, buying tickets was not an option. My budget would not allow that, as doing so would just be giving in to an expensive "want." So I had to figure out a way to get in for free. I sat by the radio and tried to win tickets during all the contest call-ins. No luck. I tried the fan-mail list, where a lucky fan would get free tickets. No luck. I had no more ideas left. Therefore, I did what any insane penny-pinching fan would do to get free tickets: I created a fake magazine.

Now, my journalistic experience was limited to a semester in college, writing comic strips and an occasional
music review for the campus paper. It was through this that
I discovered the bountiful universe of free music swag, and
usually all it took to get some was a letterhead and a fax
machine. A request to the publicity department of the
band's record label usually produced not only a free copy of
a CD for review, but often press packets, posters, T-shirts,
opportunities to interview the band—and, yes, free tickets
to nearby shows. Being a reporter (even a fake one) definitely had plenty of perks.

Extreme Cheapskate Strategy

Challenge yourself with your thriftiness. If you make saving
into a game, it will make being thrifty interesting for you.
And share your experiences with your friends and family, or
with an online community. It's very helpful to communicate
with people doing the same thing you are doing. That
means write what you are doing in a journal, or start a blog,
or just talk to your friends about it.

I wasted no time drawing up logos for *Ace NYC,* a
phony monthly publication full of reviews. After staying
late one hour at the day job, I had a bogus logo, letterhead
with the vague alliterative slogan of "Music Makes Manhattan," and business cards that transformed my residential
house into a semilegit commercial address. All it took was

adding "1st Floor" to my address. I also gave myself the title of "arts and music writer," because it sounded earnest and humble enough in case I came across any inquisitive record label peeps.

As much as I loved *Ace NYC,* I knew there was no chance in hell I was getting any access to OutKast. So I decided to focus my attention on the opening act, figuring the band's publicist would be pleasantly surprised that anyone gave a rat's ass about the group and that he'd be trying to milk the spot on the high-profile bill for all it was worth.

I called the publicity and promotions department of the band's record label and asked for a media kit and a press pass. A fax or two later, I was on the press list for Saturday night and able to see the unknown opening act and then, you know, OutKast—for free. I had done it! Creativity and some sly moves allowed me to pull it off. The show was definitely great, and I even got around to spending the $9 I had left in my weekly budget on two beers—one for me and one for a young lady I met at the show. So, overall, no one was hurt by my little dishonesty. A girl got a free beer, I'm writing about the show now, and I had the best time of my life. Sadly, for the life of me, I cannot remember the name of that opening band (or the lovely creature I kissed), but I hope they're all doing well, and I will always think of them very, very fondly. And, yes, *Ace NYC* hopes to print its first issue one of these days. I'll figure out the name of the opening band by then.

ALAN COREY 101

I like to think that making a million dollars is like losing fifty pounds: Both provide new freedoms and options to the people who achieve these goals, but neither of these objectives can be achieved overnight. Instead they're accomplished through small but crucial choices made every single day. Just like there is no product that will help you lose twenty pounds in a week, the chances that you'll make a ton of cash overnight are pretty slim (so to speak).

The key to getting rich (like losing weight) is actually amazingly simple: All you need is focused effort, self-discipline, and the right mind-set. People who stick to a plan and make good daily decisions with regard to that plan end up with amazing results. Those who don't, or those who cheat themselves, either get no results or, perhaps, even inverse results. The Billfold Blowout is just like the Weight Watchers point system that helps you track your caloric intake. You are allowed a certain budget, and you can't exceed it. If you are really good all week, you can afford to cash in your points for a cheesecake, or in my case, a cab ride and drinks. The best part is that no math is ever involved: Whatever money is left in your wallet is the money in your budget.

The key to financial success is staying focused on your goal and applying that focus to all your spending decisions. Look, no one likes to budget, and it sounds really boring, but it's the cornerstone of staying on track financially.

I was beginning to have a negative attitude about my financial situation. I knew that thinking positively had gotten me far, but eventually I realized that I had to make a change and reward myself. I had to adjust my plan, but I didn't want to give up on it altogether or detract from my overall goal of being a millionaire by thirty. My solution was to get creative and have a built-in reward program in the form of my Saturday night blowouts. Maybe that's not your thing. Maybe you don't want to live on $100 a week. That's cool. Make it $150. And then in a few weeks work your way down to $125. And then try to get to $100 eventually. But remember this: You make purchase decisions multiple times a day, and if you go into each purchase decision telling yourself that you have a spending limit and stick to it, you'll have more money than you know what to do with over time. I guarantee it.

Oh, and you're welcome to try my fake mag idea to get into shows. Just keep in mind that *Ace NYC* is taken. Who knows, maybe my 'zine will write about your band someday—I'll be in touch with your publicist.

AGE TWENTY-FOUR AND EIGHT MONTHS

Checking account: $1,000

Savings account: $0

Second, hidden savings account: $?

401(k): $10,250

Mutual fund: $5,150

Roth IRA: $6,000

Equity on apartment: $40,000

Equity on house: $1,000

Total net worth: $63,400

Chapter 16
Running for Coverage

HELLO, *thanks for coming out. I assume you are here because you want to have better control of your finances, get out of debt, learn how to invest in real estate, or just be richer overall. That's great. I'll tell you what I know about all of that. Please ask questions, plenty of questions. I don't know everything. I just know what I've done. But first I want to learn about each of you, and what brought you here, what your goals are. Thankfully, it's a small group, so take your time and share your story. No, Karl, not that story.*

My circle of friends knew that I was doing some big-time investing. They were getting my e-mails looking for tenants and such. It was as odd to them as it was to me that I was a landlord. Pretty soon my friends wanted a piece of the action too. Whenever we went out, they asked me all about it. They wanted to know where I had gotten the money to do it. They knew I was cheap, but still they were convinced I had gotten an inheritance, won the lottery, or blown the president. I explained to them all about saving a lot up front, going to open houses, and how I borrowed money from my friends and family. I probably told the same story about twenty different times to twenty different friends. I was happy to share my strategies with anyone who was truly interested. But then I was asked by friends of friends, and friends of friends of friends. Most of the people were just looking for a loophole or a slipup in my story, but a few were genuinely interested.

After a while, it got a little tiring telling the same story over and over to people I didn't even know. I decided that I would tell the story once, and if people wanted to hear how I was able to buy $560,000 worth of property for $14,600 of my own money, they could come and listen. Of course, I planned on charging a few dollars a head for my trouble.

I contacted a local comedy theater and found out that the place was empty on Sunday afternoons. I asked if I could use the space at no cost to teach a real-estate class in exchange for giving the theater a cut of what I collected at the door. They agreed. I was a little hesitant to send out **press releases** proclaiming my expertise in investing, but I knew what I had done, and it seemed to interest a lot of people.

There is no official format of a press release, so, like I always did, I just followed examples I found online. I figured the places I was sending it got hundreds of press releases a day, so mine had to stand out. I titled my press release "How to Be Richer Than Your Parents." I figured that would get them to at least read it and give the story a chance. Although "How to Be Cheaper Than Your Parents" was really what the class was about.

The press read it and, surprisingly, had no hesitation about calling me an expert. A local blog wrote about me, and I even got a write-up in the *New York Post* and *Time Out New York.* The word was out, and the New York media was calling me a "financial whiz kid." I had never thought of myself as that; I saw myself as a paranoid saver who bought property when I could—but I would be lying if I said I didn't like the attention. All it took was a press release, and the press was fooled into thinking I had skills!

Extreme Cheapskate Strategy

I would fill out comment cards at every possible fast-food restaurant. Many would follow up with complimentary food and/or gifts. My girlie complaint at a Wendy's that the bathroom was too cold resulted in an envelope containing an apology letter plus coupons for three free hamburgers. And they were right: It takes only three Wendy's hamburgers to stay warm in their bathroom. (And it kept me in there another half hour.)

Despite this mini flurry of press, the class came and went, and it was sparsely attended. I didn't mind. The people who came really wanted to learn my story, and it was very rewarding for me to help them out. I even made $200 for my three-hour class after giving the theater its kickback. So, no, the class wasn't a sold-out packed event, but if I hadn't done it—because, say, I was afraid of looking like a loser or falling flat on my face—I never would have gotten the press I did. And that press opened other doors for me.

People who read the articles were calling me up at work trying to partner with me. Other people who were already landlords got in touch to share war stories and ask for advice. Even a few long-lost friends read about me and just called to reconnect. (You know, those friends you have that aren't MySpace and Facebook savvy.) It was a pretty cool effect, and the result was that when I had enough money saved up to buy another property, I now had a Rolodex full of experts already working in real estate who wanted to be my partner, agent, or mortgage broker. The class itself turned out to be only part of the picture: Having my name out there had reaped some amazing benefits that had nothing to do with whether or not the event was standing room only or a total bust.

The experience taught me that once you get press, it's easier to get more press, and that the more people who know what you are doing, the better your opportunities become. I wasn't always wheeling and dealing. People would contact me and take me to Knicks games to chat, or they'd take me out to lunch; others just wanted to exchange some e-mails. Any and all of it was fine by me. People saw that I was doing something they wanted to do, and they wanted to pick my brain or swap ideas; and I was happy to be in the company of anyone who was interested in the same things that I was. All of it was time well spent.

ALAN COREY 101

If you have a story to tell, share it in whatever way makes you comfortable with the widest audience possible so that like-minded people can find you. If you've got a unique angle or information that people want and need, consider speaking somewhere or teaching a class. I considered myself far from an authority, but I knew what I had done, and the press decided that what I had to offer was good enough to label me an expert. All it took was a press release and an empty theater space on a Sunday afternoon, and I was introduced to a whole new network of contacts and friends, many of whom remain in my life both professionally and personally. And the experience touched off a cycle of media attention that only snowballed over time.

Maybe standing up in front of a room full of people isn't for you, or isn't for you right now. Find a smaller forum for meeting and connecting with people, like a professional organization or a local club dedicated to real-estate investing, small business ownership, or whatever your interest is. Connecting with people who are interested in the same thing you are is a great way to stay engaged with your ideas, maintain momentum and enthusiasm for the work you're doing, and build your network.

If you read about someone doing what you want to do, reach out to him or her. It's important to remember that people who are passionate about what they do love to talk about it, and that people who are successful at what they do know that good ideas and information can come from anywhere. (That is, in fact, part of the reason they're successful.)

The reality is that often parties on either side of the equation benefit. When people got in touch with me, it wasn't all about what they could get from me—I learned from them too. And lastly, if someone who's looking for your help and advice approaches you, never forget that one day you might ask for his help, or that he could be your next partner.

AGE TWENTY-FOUR, EIGHT MONTHS, AND TWO WEEKS

Checking account: $1,500

Savings account: $0

Second, hidden savings account: $?

401(k): $11,000

Mutual fund: $5,150

Roth IRA: $6,000

Equity on apartment: $40,000

Equity on house: $1,000

Total net worth: $64,650

PART IV

Howdy, Partner

Chapter 17
Smells Like
Team Spirit

THIS *place is so nice. You did all this work yourself? This is one hell of a gut renovation. Jesus H. Makeover! This house is the exact same dimensions as mine, but yours is one hundred times better. Man, you really know what you are doing. You've done this before? Yeah, I can tell. So you are into real estate too? I'm the least handy person in the world. We should totally partner up. Hey . . . wanna buy a place together?*

That was the first conversation I had with my next-door neighbor. He was a young guy like me, and he had his own real-estate strategy: He would buy a place, fix it up, and live in it for two years. After that, he would sell it. Then he'd buy another run-down house, fix it up, live in it for two years, and sell again. Get this: He didn't have a job. He just lived off the money he made by selling his house every two years. He had taught himself how to renovate, and it helped that he was a perfectionist—the place looked immaculate. But why was he moving every two years? He had to be running from the law.

I learned that in America, homeowners reap some amazing benefits when it comes to paying taxes. The **capital gains tax** on real estate exempts you from paying taxes on up to the first $250,000 that you make on the sale of a property that you have lived in at least two years, and that figure doubles if you are married. My neighbor was married, so he was exempt up to $500,000 on any profit he made on his real-estate investment, his own house. I estimated that by purchasing run-down property at a discount and selling it completely made over with high-end renovations, he was probably averaging a $350,000 payday every two years. And, of course, he didn't have to pay taxes on any of it. This guy had the best gig ever!

I didn't have the handiness to make over my own place, but I liked his work, and he liked my obsession with real estate. Plus, he had a year to kill before he could sell his place, and he was getting restless sitting at home doing nothing. I proposed that we buy a run-down place together, and he could teach me how to renovate it as we worked together. He liked the idea of not doing all the work himself for once, and, right there, we shook hands and created the first **partnership** either of us had ever had.

> **Tip:** It takes a man to admit this, but I even got a pointer from *The Oprah Winfrey Show* once, and I adopted it for myself. Anyway, she has a rule that if she really wants something, she waits twenty-four hours. If she still really wants that product, shirt, or whatever it is in twenty-four hours, then she'll buy it. Usually, the effort of going back to the store is more trouble than it's worth, leading her to conclude that she really doesn't want it that badly after all.

Since my $6,000 bathroom makeover, I had continued to learn about the benefits—and pitfalls—of different kinds of renovations. I saw this myself during my open house excursions.

I was always going to open houses, even when I didn't have any money to spend, because the more I saw, the easier it was for me to assess a property's value. I saw apartments where the owners had sunk a ton of cash into upgrading the master bedroom, but in the end, it didn't seem like they were getting much of a return on their investment. After a while, I was able to see that if I did a $5,000 kitchen renovation on a $200,000 apartment, it would look exactly like the $225,000 apartment I had seen the day before. I was recognizing deals left and right, but, once again, I didn't have any cash to make a move.

When I saw houses and apartments similar to mine, worth tens of thousands of dollars more than what I had recently paid for mine, I knew the market was changing or that I had a good deal. It ended up being both. I turned this way of accessing real estate into something I call the Corey Open House Formula (named as such because being an egomaniac like Donald Trump seems like an enjoyable pastime of the rich).

Corey Open House Formula

Target a neighborhood or area where you'd like to invest. Then go to every single open house in that neighborhood. You see the open houses of properties worth $50,000, and you see the ones worth $1 million. After about thirty to fifty open houses, you'll have a solid and accurate grasp of the current market value of real estate in the area where you're considering investing. You'll know what $90,000 buys you in this neighborhood, and you'll know what $900,000 buys you. And you keep going to open houses. You'll eventually recognize that a place that needs only a new bathroom will be worth just as much as the one down the block listed for $75,000 more. Then when you find that great undervalued bargain, you smile a big, toothy grin. That's when you know you are ready for a real-estate investment.

I had decided I wasn't going to borrow any more money until I paid back my friends and family. But now I had an amazing opportunity with my new partner. So once again I needed to find some money to take advantage of the situation, not to mention the rise in the real-estate market I was witnessing at my open house excursions.

After seeing yet another apartment near mine priced very high, the time had come: I decided I would sell my first real-estate purchase, my apartment. The value of it had skyrocketed more than I expected, and the "transitional" aspect of the neighborhood was now nonexistent. My apartment was now smack in the middle of the new "it" neighborhood, and people were hot to move there. (Not to mention that my *Real World* house was ten blocks away on the fringe of this hot neighborhood, increasing in value along with it.) I figured I would seize the chance to sell my apartment, pay off my debts, and use whatever money was left over to invest in another project with the next-door handyman.

A real-estate agent came over and appraised my converted two-bedroom apartment for $185,000! My $99,600 apartment had almost *doubled* in value in a little over two years. I knew the value of the apartment had appreciated, but to appreciate this much in such a short time was extraordinary. I put it on the market and sold it for less than my asking price, but I wanted to move quickly in case the zeal for my neighborhood quickly waned. I still made plenty of money. I had realized a good profit and didn't want to get too greedy by waiting for an even higher price.

Plus, according to the same agent, my other house had gone up in value close to $70,000 due to its proximity to this hot neighborhood.

After all was said and done, I walked away from the closing of my apartment with a check for $80,000. It was the biggest check I had ever seen, and, even better, it had my name on it. I then completely surprised my friends and family by paying off all my debts to them (including the 10 percent interest) one year ahead of schedule. That was a huge relief, and it felt really good to give them their money back. I also figured that by doing so, they'd be willing to lend me more money in the future—hopefully at a more favorable interest rate.

ALAN COREY 101

Recognize your strengths and weaknesses, and the strengths and weaknesses of others. I knew my neighbor had excellent renovation skills because I'd seen his work. I also knew he was a lot better at it than I was. Have I mentioned that I'm not really good at anything? We shared a common interest in real estate and had similar ideas about what made a neighborhood a smart place to invest our money. We were neighbors, after all. Finding partners is a great way to increase your resources, knowledge, and skills. He brought actual skills to the table, and I brought money and a willingness to learn, and in the end, we were far more effective than we would have been on our own. Our partnership enabled us to each invest less capital, as well as decrease our individual risk, because by going in together on the deal, we'd be sharing it.

Everyone knows that knowledge is power. Especially in investing. Recognizing value is a key ingredient in having the power of knowledge. The Corey Open House Formula was my specific way of figuring out real-estate value on my own, rather than just going with what a real-estate agent told me it was worth. If you can determine when to hold, when to sell, and when to buy anything of value, you have it made. Plus, the more knowledge you have, the better your position will be in any negotiation, so you can make even more money off buying the bargains and selling over-valued assets. My approach was specific to real estate, but a similar approach could be applied to buying cars, art, or whatever your niche interest may be.

AGE TWENTY-FIVE

Checking account: $50,000

Savings account: $0

Second, hidden savings account: $?

401(k): $11,500

Mutual fund: $5,150

Roth IRA: $6,000

Equity on house: $71,000 ($475,000 new estimated value – $404,000 mortgage)

Total net worth: $143,650

Chapter 18
Perfect Pitch

JEEZ, *this place is on the verge of collapse. Yes, that probably means it's cheap too. But the renovation expenses would be really high. Then again, this location is great. Maybe we could find some investors . . . somewhere. Wow, if this family doesn't move out soon, they could die. The floors are about to buckle! How long have they lived like this? Let's get out of here! Jesus H. Hardhat, that place was dangerous—but perfect. We have to get it!*

My new partner and I had found a building. It was in a prime location called Red Hook, in what we predicted would be Brooklyn's next up-and-coming neighborhood. The area was still kind of gritty, but it was close to the water, and the neighborhood had a lot of charm to it. Both of us thought it was just a matter of time before the real estate in the neighborhood became hot.

The building was also loaded with potential because it was in need of a major renovation, and we knew that by buying a decrepit place and fixing it up ourselves, we could make a lot of money. It was a mixed-use building with a store and two apartments above it. We figured we could gut-renovate it for $200,000 and then either rent it out or sell it. It was a **for sale by owner,** and they were asking $500,000 for it.

We both knew that for the shape the place was in, that was way too much. A $500,000 price tag plus a $200,000 renovation budget was way beyond what we could pay, even though we assumed we could still make money in that scenario. A similar fully renovated building in the area was selling for $900,000, and we knew we could get close to that price range after a full renovation. Regardless, neither one of us had enough money to embark on a $700,000 project. We had to either find a third partner with a lot of money or get the owners to come down on the price—most likely, we had to do both.

The day after we saw the house, I flew to Las Vegas for a bachelor party. Fat Matt, who had loaned me $10,000 to buy my house, was about to get married, and I had to be there to mark the big step *he* was about to take. But in the back of my mind, I couldn't get that property out of my head. Yes, it was in complete disrepair, but we were going to rip everything out of it anyway and bring the whole building back to life. I needed the owners to lower the price drastically, and I needed to find us a third partner. As is often the case with real estate in New York City, I had to do both quickly.

As everyone was arriving for the three-day debauchery weekend, I sat by the swimming pool making calls. It was ridiculous. I felt like I was in a movie: I was twenty-six, poolside at a Las Vegas casino, trying to make a half-million-dollar business deal on my cell phone. All I was missing was a martini, a masseuse, and a nickel-plated revolver under a silk robe. It felt pretty cool, but it would only be really cool if I could actually pull it off.

I called the owners of the building and explained to them the scary condition of their floors. They seemed to know already, and I assumed that's why they were looking to sell. I told them the property was probably worth $375,000. Of course, I thought it was worth more, but I figured it was worth a shot, especially if they weren't willing to put the money into repairing the building. I was expecting them to hang up the phone on me right there, but they didn't. Like most homeowners, they had a certain attachment to their house (they had lived in it for forty years), and they wanted the next occupant to be someone they liked. They didn't want the place to be torn down or the original character of the building to change. (These preferences are usually shielded by a real-estate agent to prevent any deal from falling through, but this was for sale by the owner, and I had to deal with them directly.) I told them the truth: We really wanted the place, and our goal was to make it beautiful again. I ended the call with an offer of $390,000, and they seemed to take the news of my lowball offer pretty well. They said they'd think it over and get back to me.

I had to find someone else who might be interested in investing in the project. I called my girlfriend (she still being interested in me post–*Queer Eye* makeover and, thus, now a long-term girlfriend) and told her about what I was trying to piece together. The only person she knew who might be interested was her father. I figured that would be a good place to start before I touched base with other potential partners.

I had met her dad a few times, once at my televised faux cocktail party on *Queer Eye,* and he always liked talking to me about real estate. I also knew he was a high-powered lawyer, so he probably had the capital I needed. It wasn't lost on me that if he became a third party in our partnership, he could probably give us plenty of free legal advice too, which is never a bad thing. I gave him a call and proposed the deal to him complete with a pitch about the building, my neighbor's amazing work, and our feelings about the changes ahead for the neighborhood. He seemed somewhat interested and told me to follow up with him when I had some concrete numbers. I had a maybe; I could definitely work with a maybe.

Extreme Cheapskate Strategy

Consider being a model at a school for hair stylists to get cuts for free. Obviously, you don't want to do anything crazy or complicated, but (a) these people aren't total morons and (b) they want to do a great job. It's their "class work," and they don't want to get a D plus. And you don't need a haircut every month. It's okay to wait awhile.

Later that day, the owners of the building called me back and gave me a counteroffer: They would sell it for $400,000. Lowballing had worked once again! (I figured they might come down a little bit, but a $100,000 price cut was amazing.) I had no choice but to say yes and take the deal. We had an oral agreement on the phone, but that doesn't mean much. I had to finalize the rest, figure out how it could get done logistically, and get an agreement in writing. This was too good to pass up.

I called back my girlfriend's father and pitched him the scenario. As equal partners, the three of us would each invest $100,000. The building was partly zoned as commercial, so the bank would require us to put down a 20 percent deposit. That meant $80,000 of our total $300,000 budget would be used for our down payment. We'd spend the remaining $220,000 on renovations, mortgage payments, and budget overruns. We estimated it would take six months to do all the work, and then we could rent it out for some monthly income or most likely sell the place for around $900,000. If our plan worked to perfection, we would each make a profit of around $93,333. (This is how the numbers fell out: purchase price of $400,000 + $220,000 budget = $620,000. Sell for $900,000, leaving us with a $280,000 profit, which we would split three ways, giving us $93,333 each.)

Fortunately, the numbers looked good to my girlfriend's father too, and he agreed to join us. So my neighbor had $100,000 to put in the deal, our new partner had $100,000 to put in the deal—but I had only the $50,000 in my checking account. I kept that last part to myself. I saw my golden ticket, and I would just have to find a way to get $50,000. I had done it once before, and I figured I could find a way to pull it off one more time. If I were successful, I would make $93,333! I had to find a way to get the deal done.

ALAN COREY 101

Be a deal maker. Always be on the lookout for a way to make things work. I didn't want to pass on a property because it was priced too high; I wanted to pass on a property because it was a bad investment. I worked every possible angle to make it even more attractive to all parties involved. I talked the owners into a $100,000 price cut. I was an enthusiastic pitchman to win over my girlfriend's father. If those two things didn't work out, I had other strategies. I was going to ask the owners if they were willing to defer payment until after renovations (most likely a no, but I was running low on options). I could have maybe sold my two-family house if the numbers worked or started looking for a fourth partner. I was determined to get this deal done. I saw the money that could be made, and I wasn't going to let it slip by. The deal was coming together, which I made happen. I just had to come up with my end of the bargain, another $50,000. I knew I could rely on myself, as I was the final piece to the puzzle.

AGE TWENTY-SIX

Checking account: $52,500

Savings account: $0

Second, hidden savings account: $? (I didn't check the amount for the New Year; I didn't want to know.)

401(k): $13,500

Mutual fund: $7,150

Roth IRA: $10,000 (At the time, $4,000 was the maximum contribution for one year.)

Equity on house: $71,000

Total net worth: $154,150

Chapter 19
Home: A Loan

HMM, *I could sell my house. The profit would give me enough to complete the deal on the new building. I can't sell the house, it's a cash cow for me. Jesus H. Udders, this is one big dairy cow of money. Plus, I'd still need a place to live! I could hit up my friends and family again, maybe even other friends and family. But even though I know I would pay them back, it'll still stress me out. Maybe I could get a legit second job? Maybe I could get a loan. Hmm . . . I wonder how loans work? Um, I should get right on that.*

I figured I'd start at my bank to try getting some money, so I scheduled an appointment with the loan coordinator at my branch. I was pretty nervous, as I didn't know what to expect. I dressed nicely too, which I think is always a good idea when you're about to ask someone for money. (Okay, so I just combed my hair. But that's better than nothing.) I sat down with a guy wearing a tie, and I explained my situation to him. He listened and was very encouraging about my entrepreneurial spirit. He explained that if I indeed had the $71,000 in equity in my house that

I claimed I did, I would qualify for a **home equity** loan or a home equity line of credit (HELOC) for the $50,000 I needed.

HELOCs work exactly like a credit card, except that you withdraw money from your account with checks. In my case, I would have a credit limit of $50,000 and a stack of checks to write against that amount for whatever I wanted. Each month I would get a bill, and I would have to pay off my debt and the interest that came with it a little bit at a time. A home equity loan is very similar, but instead of having a credit line to draw from, I would get all $50,000 up front and then slowly pay it off each month along with the interest I owed on it. I liked the freedom of being able to write checks in different amounts when necessary, so I went with the HELOC.

In essence, I was trading my equity for the loan. If I defaulted on the loan, the bank could sell my house to get the $50,000 I owed it, in what is called a **foreclosure**. On the other hand, if I made my loan payments on time and paid off the money I had borrowed, all the equity was mine again. I wasn't about to lose my house, so I made damn sure I wasn't going to default on the loan.

Cashing in on equity can be a very risky move, and it's not for everyone, since my backup plan was once again a worst-case scenario. If the bank did have to foreclose on my home, it would get the $50,000 that I owed plus all the extra equity that came with the house. Envisioning this was hard to do; my house was a crucial cog in my millionaire wheel. It was earning me passive income in a major way and providing me with a place to live. But cashing in on its equity was necessary if I wanted to complete the next deal. If things went sour, and I couldn't make my mortgage payments, foreclosure would be inevitable. I had to analyze exactly what I was risking. Was I willing to risk most of what I had gained, a major portion of my net worth for this one new investment? After thinking it out, preparing myself for the worst, and doing some soul searching, I had my answer. This deal wasn't for everyone, but it was for me. I had done my homework, and I knew this next deal would be profitable. After thinking it all out, I was even more motivated to keep moving forward on the deal. In my mind, the reward would be worth all the effort, and I was okay with risking it all. It wasn't a gamble, it was an educated risk.

> **Tip:** Never, ever pay full price. Need a dress for a wedding? A suit for a new job? Head to one of those mega outlet malls (don't pretend you don't know what I'm talking about), shop at discount retailers like Marshalls, T. J. Maxx, Daffy's, Filene's Basement, or Syms—and be sure to comb the clearance racks. Just don't do what I did and brag about how cheap your clothes were while you're on a date!

So I went forward with the HELOC. To complete the process, I had to fill out a few forms, verify my income, and get my house appraised by the bank. (They weren't just going to take my word on the value of it.) A week later the appraiser was walking around my property, taking pictures and measurements, and getting a tour of the place. He was impossible to read. I didn't know if he liked the place, if he was familiar with the changes in the neighborhood, or if he was just having a bad day. I was nervous. If the appraisal came in lower than I thought, I wouldn't be able to borrow the full $50,000, and time was running out before the owners might find another buyer for their property.

A few days later, I got a call from the same banker in a tie, and he had great news. I had gotten approved for the HELOC! To add to my good fortune, my house was appraised for an even higher value than I anticipated: $510,000! (That meant a loan of more than $50,000 was available for me.) I met him the next day, signed some papers, and I had access to $60,000 whenever I needed it. I could complete the deal with my partners!

ALAN COREY 101

Assess all your options. I didn't even know that you could take out loans based on your home equity, but I'm glad I found out, because it was the key to getting the capital I needed for my next deal. By figuring out all of my options (and asking a lot of questions), I was able to achieve what I wanted: finding $50,000. If you're motivated and confident enough, you'll uncover ways to get what you want. I say this because I did it time and time again, and with each development I found a new solution to essentially the same problem: getting money. The key was that every step of the way, I made smart financial decisions, took calculated risks, and was able to increase my overall assets. The end result was that each time I needed capital, I had more to offer lenders than what I'd had when I approached them before.

It never hurts to talk to a bank. Borrowing money from a bank is yet another reason why you should aim to have the highest credit score possible. Your credit rating may be a decisive factor in whether or not you get a loan you desperately need, and it will certainly affect the interest rate you pay if you are approved. Whatever you do, whenever you borrow money, make sure that you will have the funds to make the payments on the loan. Defaulting on a loan will cost you even more money and will land you in far worse shape than if you had never borrowed the money in the first place.

Lastly, recognize the worst-case scenario that could occur whenever you make a major financial decision. I was taking a big risk, and, admittedly, I was a bit zealous about this deal (especially after the poolside Vegas scene). However, I was mentally prepared for an apocalyptic life of working two jobs and losing all I had gained to get it done. This had the side effect of being a motivational tool, but it also helped me in understanding the risks. If I was willing to do that and still move forward, then I knew it was the right choice.

AGE TWENTY-SIX AND ONE MONTH
Checking account: $53,500
Savings account: $0
**Second, hidden savings account: $? (I didn't
check the amount for the New Year; I didn't
want to know.)**
401(k): $14,100
Mutual fund: $7,150
Roth IRA: $10,000
**Equity on house: $50,000 ($510,000 value –
$400,000 mortgage – $60,000 HELOC =
$50,000)**
Total net worth: $134,750

Chapter 20
Flipping Out

DEMOLITION *is the best stress reliever! I get to take a sledge-hammer to a wall and just beat the hell out of it; I get to take a crowbar to a window; I get to be completely sweaty and filthy—all in the name of home improvement. I can't wait to do it again to-morrow. But the day's done; time to go get a beer across the street.*

We demolished everything because we had to.

The previous owners had been extremely creative when it came to maximizing the space they had. I believe ten people had lived in a building originally designed to be two one-bedroom apartments and a store. The store itself had been converted into extra bedrooms to help accommodate the number of residents.

Beyond that, the problems were many. My new invest-ment made the Munsters' house look like the Playboy Man-sion. The stairs to the landing had no railing, and each step was a different height. As an added bonus, the entire flight of stairs was covered with repugnant green linoleum. Puke was the only accurate way to describe its color. Every room featured hideous, bulging drop ceilings, and all of them were marred by yellow and brown ring marks, thanks to decades of pooling water, maybe even urine.

There were signs of half-assed attempts at fixing a leaky roof: We found antique aluminum beer signs nailed into random spots on the top floor's ceilings. This technique had clearly never stopped the leaks, it just diverted the incoming water to a well-placed bucket. Awesome.

In one of the bathrooms, we found a ten-inch hole in the shower wall that had rusted around the waterspout, and it looked like no effort had ever been made to fix the problem. A situation like this could easily lead to water flowing down to the floor beams, which would completely soak and warp them. A month of this could buckle the floors, but it was pretty clear that this had probably been happening for years.

Every room I entered, I hit my head on the doorway, but in the middle of each room, I could stand up straight. The slopes of the floor were like none I had ever seen. If I were a skateboarder, I would have been ecstatic: This house had several built-in half-pipes. But I was not a skater, I was an investor, so it had to go.

It ended up being a complete strip-down. We removed all the walls, the ceilings, and the floorboards. We took out the beams, stairs, and years of accumulated trash stockpiled in the attic and crawl spaces. A complete gut renovation.

When we were done, it was a shell of a building where a disaster zone once stood. We had no choice but to do it this way—it was the only safe way to renovate the place.

In the end, we gave the building a brand-new life. We returned it to its original layout, and made it two one-bedroom apartments and a store. Our goal was to create a building that would wow someone and that would stay standing another seventy years or more.

We installed brand-new oak hardwood floors in each unit, and even got a great discount on them because we bought in bulk. Each apartment featured an exposed brick wall, which not only saved us some cash on having to install drywall, but also added loads of character to the place. Granite countertops, custom-built cabinets, and modern pocket doors in both apartments completed the luxurious feel we wanted the building to have, and we installed space-saving and energy-saving tankless water heaters. The place looked amazing! I wanted to move in myself.

The whole process of renovating took about nine months to complete—not the six we had estimated—and I spent many weekends working on the project with my partner. It was brutal, hard work, and it essentially became a second job, but I knew that in the end it would all be worth it. If everything went according to plan, I might even be able to quit my day job.

The project ended up draining us of the $220,000 in capital we'd pulled together. While we were frustrated by our three-month delay, that extra time actually benefited us, as the neighborhood renaissance we'd predicted was shifting into high gear, and the value of the property just continued to climb. We even kidded ourselves that maybe we could get a million dollars for the building.

Before we even decided whether we were going to rent it out or sell it, we had an offer on the place for $900,000. A group of guys had swung by during renovations, liked the building, and wanted to jump on it before anyone else could. The hardest part of selling a building is finding a buyer, and here we had one on our doorstep midrenovation. We agreed to a $900,000 deal. Quick and easy. My partners and I celebrated and congratulated one another for a job well done. The victory, however, was short lived. The would-be buyers kept stalling and stalling, and they never signed the paperwork. After about six weeks of patiently waiting for them to get their act together, we told them we had to move on. We couldn't waste any more time. Having already received the offer we had been shooting for, we decided to go ahead and sell the building instead of trying to rent it out. Other potential buyers would probably offer the same. Plus, we'd exhausted our budget and wanted to make our money back in one lump sum rather than in monthly installments. Things were tight; we wanted our money sooner rather than later.

Operating under the principle of "Hey, you never know if you don't try," we contacted the number-one real-estate firm in New York City, the Corcoran Group, to see if it would be interested in selling the place for us. The Corcoran Group is about as serious as you can get when it comes to New York City real estate. It represents all kinds of property, but its stable of offerings includes $8 million lofts in SoHo, $12 million penthouse apartments overlooking Central Park, $15 million townhouses on the Upper West

Side, and, you know, $20 million estates in Miami Beach. The Corcoran Group even brokered the Louisiana Purchase—okay, just kidding, but you get the idea. So there was a certain amount of cachet involved with having Corcoran represent our building, but on a practical level we also really needed an agency that could hook us up with someone who had $900,000 ready to spend. It seemed like a pretty safe bet in that regard.

A slick, blond, power-suit-wearing Corcoran rep somehow teleported into our rough-around-the-edges (if not cozy) enclave of Brooklyn and checked out our baby. After a quick walk-through, she told us that she thought she could sell it for $1.1 million. Say what? $1.1 million! We were skeptical, but she was confident, so we signed an **exclusive agreement** with the agency and planned to have an open house that weekend.

Once again, we were ecstatic, and we celebrated with more beers at the bar across the street. $1.1 million! If we got that, our payday would be $160,000 each! We figured it was a long shot that someone would offer that much, but it was still nice to think about.

Two days later we got a call from the agent saying she had an offer for $1 million. She told my partner (who was her main point person) that the interested party was a **solid buyer**—so much so that she wasn't even going to list our building on the company's Web site. I'm certainly not one to turn down a million dollars, but I was a little confused. What happened to the $1.1 million that she was so confident we could pull off? I told my partner to dig deeper.

Yeah, well, he did:

"Alan."

"Yeah."

"I found out who wants to buy our building."

"Yeah?"

"It's Barbara Corcoran." (This is approximately the point in the conversation where I shit my pants.)

The agent had explained that this was what she called a "unique" circumstance. This buyer wasn't just any buyer. It was her boss, the founder and CEO of the Corcoran Group, Ms. Barbara Corcoran herself. This person was known as "the female Donald Trump" until she made a name for herself. And a big name at that. Unique buyer indeed. One of the richest women in New York wanted to buy our building for her own *personal* investment!

After picking ourselves up off the floor, we were scratching our heads. Why did multimillionaire real-estate diva Barbara Corcoran want to buy our building here in gritty Red Hook? Did she know something we didn't know? Should we keep it and not sell? Did she know that we'd bought it for only $400,000 less than a year ago? And why was Barbara's offer only $1 million?

With my partner serving as the face of our enterprise, I had the luxury of being slightly removed from the negotiations, which also enabled me to be a little more objective about the whole thing. (He was, understandably, freaking out.) I convinced him we should counteroffer with our planned asking price of $1.1 million, reasoning that the place hadn't even been posted on Corcoran's traffic-heavy

Web site. Doing so would buy us some time to make a decision, plus we knew that Megabucks Barbara had an extra $100,000 lying around if she really wanted the place. As it turned out, she did. She accepted the counteroffer and was ready to close in an **all cash deal.**

About a month later, we finally closed on the place, and the three of us took home more than we had initially planned when we first hatched our scheme. After some closing fees and the **real-estate agent's fee,** we each walked away from the deal with around $150,000! In a final surreal twist, on the day after the closing, the front page of the *New York Times* real-estate section featured a full-blown color picture of Barbara Corcoran standing outside our newly renovated building (although, officially, I guess it was actually hers now). The accompanying article explained how Barbara considered the purchase a long-term investment for her personal investment portfolio, and that she saw great things on the horizon for the neighborhood. And so did I.

ALAN COREY 101

Trust your own knowledge, as you could be just as good as or better than the experts in one area, like finding the next great location. But you should also recognize when the experts do indeed know more than you do in another area, such as in pricing and selling your home.

My partners and I had been right all along. Here was a

seasoned veteran, Barbara Corcoran, a star in the field of finding the next hot neighborhood, and she was verifying that my twenty-six-year-old instincts were right. (OMG! I might have a skill! Nah, I was probably just lucky.) We had spotted the beginning of a shift exactly one year before she had, and because of that, we profited handsomely. (From her, no less.) Our only miscalculation and admitted weakness, it seemed, was that we didn't know as much as the pros as far as selling price.

Identify the leaders in your industry and try to get them involved with your projects. Why *not* approach the best people out there? The worst they can say is no. The Corcoran Group had a history of selling properties like ours, had a lot of exposure in the tristate area, and boasted a Rolodex of platinum contacts. Yes, we had to give the agency a small cut, but it sold our building for $200,000 more than we would have. Our strategy for **flipping property** brought us big payouts.

As hard as it is, it's important to keep your emotions out of any kind of negotiation. To say we were ecstatic about Barbara Corcoran's initial bid on our building is a huge understatement, but if we had gotten swept away in the excitement, we never would have seen that $1.1 million cash deal. When we looked at the situation objectively, it made sense to find out what other buyers might offer us and to assume that Barbara could cough up the cash if she was serious. Like a true pro, she was lowballing us, but if she could negotiate, we could negotiate right back.

Also, it's important to remember that no deal is finalized

without signatures. We could have settled with a handshake agreement with the original "buyers"; unfortunately, verbal commitments don't make for a solid deal closer. We could have gotten in trouble if we had waited for this stalling group of investors. We made sure from that point on that without any deal in writing, we weren't going to proceed with celebrations, no matter how much we all liked beer.

AGE TWENTY-SIX AND NINE MONTHS

Checking account: $153,500

Savings account: $0

Second, hidden savings account: $?

401(k): $19,300

Mutual fund: $9,000 (stocks rose in value)

Roth IRA: $10,500 (stocks rose in value)

Equity on house: $110,000 (paid off my

HELOC; $510,000 value – $400,000 mortgage)

Total net worth: $302,300

PART V

Taking It to the House

Chapter 21
Silent, but Deadly Profitable

OKAY, *that worked out! You guys up for another one? Let's start hitting some open houses and see where the next million-dollar building is. What, you want to add a fourth partner? Are you sure? Okay, he'll help with the renovations and make the flip go a little quicker? Can't argue with that. And he already found a building? Well, it all sounds good to me!*

This project was so successful for the three of us, we were excited to keep rolling along with the plan to flip another property together. By this time, I had broken up with my girlfriend (okay, I got dumped), but of course her dad still liked to make money. (Plus, I was very friendly with her whole family.) We three partners decided we had to do it again. But now it was pretty clear that we couldn't do it in the same neighborhood of Red Hook, Brooklyn. The press, not to mention the presence of Barbara, made real-estate values skyrocket in the area. Conveniently, a person we had hired to help us renovate our last building approached one of my partners about working with us. He wanted to be a fourth partner in our next deal and, to sweeten the offer, he had already found a building that would make us some money.

He had set his sights on a neighborhood that bordered the one where I'd bought my first apartment. My old neighborhood of Clinton Hill, Brooklyn, was as hot as ever, and its adjacent areas were now transitioning at a rapid pace. Everywhere you looked, there were buildings undergoing renovation, new restaurants, and new stores. We knew the synergy of all the changes and investments would have a big impact, especially if we were selling a building that was freshly renovated.

With the help of the Corey Open House Formula (man, I love the name of that), we verified that his find was a good deal. It was a two-family brownstone about the same size as the mixed-use building we had just sold. It was also within fifteen blocks of my current house, the market value of which was continuing to soar. The "it" neighborhood had officially made all the surrounding areas equally hot. However, this new place we were looking at also needed a gut renovation, and it had an asking price of $650,000. We saw the same potential in this property, estimating that we could put in another $200,000 in renovations and sell it for around $1,100,000.

Surprise: I didn't have all the capital to do the full deal once again. But *this* time, it was because I was investing in other projects too, not because I didn't actually have any money. My solution was to sign on for a 17 percent partnership in this renovation, instead of the usual equal cut, which was now 25 percent each for the four of us. I would put in less money to get the deal done, and then I'd step back and not do any work. I would just be a silent partner. In return, I'd get a smaller cut of the deal after we sold the property. The deal definitely worked best for me, and it seemed to work for everyone else too.

Eight months later, with the help of the same slick real-estate agent at the Corcoran Group, we sold our newly renovated building to one of director Spike Lee's right-hand men for $1.3 million! The result was another $200,000 increase from the profit we initially projected. Our underestimating our potential was becoming a trend. The best part was that I made $76,500 on the deal for not doing anything! *I* now had the best gig ever! It seemed the rich really do get richer. I liked finally being on that side of the equation. It made the finish line even closer.

After celebrating the New Year, along with my twenty-seventh birthday, I looked over my finances. To be sure, things were going great, but I took some big hits paying an ungodly amount of taxes on the selling of a building. I wondered what I'd still need to reach my million-dollar destination.

This was the overall picture: I had recently celebrated my fourth anniversary at the day job, and had gotten my yearly bonus and a raise to $52,000. I wasn't paying any rent because I was still living for free in my house, and I was earning the rental income from it. Around that time, a nearby building the same size as my house sold for

$799,000, which raised the market value of my property (and my equity, as I had paid only $450,000) right along with it. Finally, the strategy of investing in run-down properties in up-and-coming neighborhoods and bringing them back to life turned all of our lives upside down. We were making a lot of money and fairly quickly. This all meant that I was getting much, much closer to a million dollars.

ALAN COREY 101

It doesn't hurt to play a minority role in a deal. I would have loved to have been a 25 percent equal partner, but the timing of the deal wasn't working out perfectly. Rather than just saying no outright, I offered a reduced cut along with a reduced role in the next flip. It paid off, as for basically no effort, I made over $75,000! I didn't have any input in the type of floors, the cabinets, and so forth, that went into the house, but I had other things to worry about. And it was in all of my partners' best interest to do the best job they could do, as their money was fully invested in the project too. They had my full trust, and it played out perfectly.

Let's not forget the benefits of adding a fourth partner. He created his own worth by providing a great property he'd found. And he added free labor to the deal, which resulted in a quicker sale of the building by a full month. He created his own opportunity and we benefited from it.

With three years left to reach my goal, my current breakdown was:

AGE TWENTY-SEVEN

Checking account: $245,000

Savings account: $0

Second, hidden savings account: $?

401(k): $24,100

Mutual fund: $14,150

Roth IRA: $14,500

Equity on house: $375,000 ($775,000 new market value – $400,000 mortgage – $0 HELOC [loan paid off] = $375,000)

Total net worth: $672,750

Chapter 22
Bar Tender

IS *it time to quit my job? I guess I don't need it anymore. But why?*
It hasn't gotten in the way of my accomplishing the things I wanted
to do. What am I saying? I'm not a millionaire yet—I need to keep
earning as much as possible until I am. Plus, it's nice getting full
health insurance. And a steady job does make it a little easier to get
a mortgage. I'm definitely sick of answering phones all day, but the
job has helped me when times were tough, and I need to make sure I
have a good footing somewhere. It's too bad no one calls just to
chitchat anymore. Those were the good old days. Ah yes, day one.

Pretty much everyone thought I was completely insane
to keep my day job, but I decided I would stay until I
reached my goal of being a millionaire by thirty. Old habits
die hard. I remained thrifty and I didn't go out and reward
myself with a big-ticket item like a plasma-screen TV or a
new wardrobe, like a lot of people who had $245,000 in
their checking account would have done. I continued using
the same TV I'd had since eighth grade, and I didn't even
buy one new shirt. I even remained committed to my an-

nual ritual of talking myself out of purchasing an iPod by saying, "They'll come out with a better one next year." The way I saw it, any of those purchases would just keep me at my job longer, because they'd be a step backward on my path to being a millionaire.

However, I did reward myself, albeit in a financially nerdy way: I **refinanced** my mortgage.

Interest rates were at an all-time low, and I wanted to take advantage of that. I got a new loan at an interest rate 2 percent lower than the rate on my first one. It cost me $10,000 to refinance my mortgage after loan fees, appraisal fees, and other miscellaneous expenses, but my new thirty-year fixed mortgage was saving me an extra $1,000 a month! I'd make up that expense in less than a year. Overall, this was much better than a flat-screen TV. Plus, the reduction in my monthly mortgage allowed me to make some much-needed changes at home too.

After a few years of *Real World* insanity, I changed my seven-bedroom single-family house back into a two-family. It once again became its originally intended layout: one unit of three bedrooms and another unit of three bedrooms plus my office-cum-bedroom. Sure, it meant a little less rental income, but it also meant fewer headaches. I didn't have to worry about individual roommate squabbles, collecting six separate rent checks, and finding a tenant who would fit in with *all* the personalities living in my house. Instead, the tenants in the other half of the house would be responsible for finding their own roommates, resolving their own squabbles, and providing me with one rent check. I would just have to worry about myself and the three room-mates in my half of the house. It reduced the workload on my shoulders, for sure, and I was willing to take a $200 cut in rental income in order to reduce the stress in my life.

I also spent about $25,000 renovating the backyard, the basement, and my front stoop. While it was a chunk of change, all of the improvements would make the building comparable to another house on the block that was selling for $800,000. I was sitting pretty, financially speaking, but I wasn't ready to be too conservative just yet. I was still young and looking to make big gains; just as important, I wanted to have some more fun.

I was also thinking about the bar across the street from my former building in Red Hook. My partners and I used to head there after working hard all day on the renovation. Beer had never tasted so good. Every time we walked in, the owner was sitting alone behind the bar, and he was always extremely grateful we were there. It seemed like business was always slow. I, for one, couldn't understand it. From the first time I saw the bar, I knew it was a place I was going to fall in love with fast. It reflected the feel of the neighbor-hood and was just overrun with rustic charm. The bar was filled with old-school intimate brown vinyl booths, but it was also perfect for large, boisterous gatherings of friends.

Black-and-white photos of people long since dead hung on the walls with no rhyme or reason, but they added a unique feel to the space. Mismatched antique lamps with homemade shades hung above the bar, rounding out the unpretentious anyone-is-welcome atmosphere. It was pretty much everything I would ever want in a bar if I were to open one myself: a place to drink solo and leave the night with new friends, or somewhere eclectic and out of the norm to take a date.

The truth was, I *had* always wanted to open a bar, and I knew the owner was frustrated by his lack of business. (We had gotten to know him pretty well because we were always there.) You'll remember that eventually I *also* knew that Barbara Corcoran was eyeing the neighborhood as one of the next big things, and I figured it was only a matter of time until a media and development blitz went down. I kept that bit of information to myself, and I asked the owner if he was interested in selling the bar.

He didn't take long to respond, saying he wouldn't let the place go for anything less than $100,000. My numbers showed it was probably worth that. I bought it for $80,000. This was the "other project" I was working on, and the reason why I had to take the minority role in the last flip we did.

Tip: If real estate doesn't interest you, you can educate yourself online about stocks. There are plenty of Web sites that break down and explain stocks; the Motley Fool (www.fool.com), CNN-Money (www.money.com), and Morningstar (www.morningstar.com) are great places to start. These are, in fact, among the places where I taught myself.

I found a partner to go in on the bar with me, a friend with not as much capital as me, but who was a culinary whiz. We agreed that I'd put in more money up front, and we'd turn the place into a bar/restaurant that he would oversee on a day-to-day basis. We both were from the South, so we opted for a menu of our favorite food: Southern barbecue.

I wanted to leave everything that initially attracted me to the bar in the first place as it was. And we did. However, I also wanted to emphasize our new barbecue menu and mix in a little down-home Southern flair to the charm the place already had. I decorated a couple of park benches using my collection of license plates and placed the benches on the sidewalk out front. To the back room that had a pool table, we added a TV to appease the local sports nuts. We fastened an old-fashioned flashing neon Bar-B-Q sign above the door, and the place screamed cozy barbecue shack. We even changed the name from Pioneer Bar (it was on the corner of Pioneer Street, after all) to Pioneer Bar-B-Q.

By keeping all the signage and decorations put up by the last owner, we didn't alienate the existing clientele, and the locals still came around. After some positive write-ups in a few newspapers, people were traveling to our hole-in-the-wall restaurant from all five boroughs. Thanks to some insider knowledge, plus some personal touches and hard work, business changed dramatically with just a few minor changes to the restaurant.

Our best day to date was on a recent Fourth of July,

when people sat in the backyard beer garden and drank until sundown. A block away, on the waterfront, you could see the fireworks in Manhattan and a docked *Queen Mary 2* ocean liner. (A new commercial port had opened— something I also knew was in the works, thanks to having read a few news reports about it.) After the fireworks show, everyone came back and continued hanging out. A year before, the same bar sat empty with just me and my partners wiping our faces after a three-day weekend of renovating. In just one year, business had increased drastically, profits were on the rise, and we haven't looked back since. (Plus, now I have a place to eat and drink for free whenever I want.)

Ironically, as I continued to get press for the different projects I was involved in, people around the office at my day job started asking me how I managed to pull it off. Even upper management was coming to me and asking my advice about personal finance. Whenever I explained my financial game plan to them, my story of pinching pennies bored them to death. They wanted some trick. Some secret. It's not exciting or all that complicated, I'd say, but it is what worked for me. There had to be a reason these people were coming to me for advice. I could only assume that I was financially better off than some of them. Or at least better prepared for my future. Probably a bit of both.

ALAN COREY 101

Similar to my Billfold Blowouts, I still found ways to reward myself without hurting my overall goal. I spent $10,000 to refinance my mortgage, but the expense saved me $1,000 a month in the long term. I spent $25,000 in renovations, but that move raised the value of my home. And, finally, I was in a position to follow a dream of mine, and I made the reward of owning a bar and restaurant work in my favor financially, because it wasn't just a toy, it was a business investment. (Even if I never made a dime on the place, I could always sell it for at least what I had paid for it.) I was rewarding myself without sacrificing all I had gained. Free beer makes for a great reward, no doubt about it.

If you aren't happy, you won't remain on target to reach your goals. You have to accept the sacrifices you make and see the good in them. I almost dropped out of college to open up a bar, because it was something I always wanted to do. When I told my mom my plan back then, she cried for two weeks. So I decided to graduate from college first (wise move) and then told myself I'd pursue it at a later date (hopefully at a time that wouldn't bring my mother to tears). I knew I would, I just didn't know when. I recognized the frustrated bar owner was the pathway to achieving that dream. Plus, it didn't hurt having some insider knowledge to sweeten the deal. I knew I would regret passing up the chance again, and so I seized the opportunity.

AGE TWENTY-SEVEN AND FIVE MONTHS

Checking account: $180,000

Savings account: $0

Second, hidden savings account: $?

401(k): $28,900

Mutual fund: $16,475

Roth IRA: $15,800

Equity on house: $400,000

Equity on bar and restaurant: $50,000 (after our minor changes)

Total net worth: $691,175

Chapter 23
Boomtown, USA

JESUS H. *Mortgage, the house down the street just sold for $900,000! Didn't that guy buy that house for $750,000 last year?? Damn! And look, this house for sale in the paper shows the square footage is half the size of my house, and it's selling for $900,000! Things are out of control! I've gotta find out what my house is worth.*

Over the next seven months, I got extremely lucky. The surging real-estate market kept soaring, and the value of my biggest investment, my house, went up right along with it. This booming real-estate market was happening all across the United States, not just in New York City. Everyone was making out big. I was able to benefit from what was truly an exceptional circumstance that no one really had expected—record lows in interest rates meant skyrocketing home prices. I was in a position to win big just because I was a homeowner.

To explain fully, the poor performance of the nation's

economy after 2001 meant that interest rates of all kinds, including mortgage rates, were continually being cut. Over the next five years, every few months new record lows in rates were being created by the feds. They wanted—actually needed—citizens to borrow large portions of money and spend it in order to help restart the economy. The best way to do that was to make it cheap to borrow money. And their plan worked. These record lows in mortgage interest rates meant more people could now afford to buy a house. And buy houses they did. It created a frenzied demand to purchase a home, resulting in the prices for homes going way, way up.

In New York City, it wasn't unheard of for property to double in value in less than a year. It was actually the norm. Many stories in the papers told of people selling their homes and taking early retirement because of the newfound treasure of equity they had in their homes. For instance, during this time I saw the value of my house go up $187,000 in less than a year! Just for doing nothing. I was merely a homeowner in an exploding real-estate market.

> **Tip:** Different investment options have different levels of risk too. Bonds are the safest, stocks are riskier (but higher risk usually means a chance at a higher return), and within stocks, some are riskier than others—for example, international or emerging market stocks tend to carry a higher risk than domestic ones. In the same way, buying a mutual fund or *exchange-traded fund* (a portfolio of many different stocks) protects you more than buying individual stocks, because if one stock tanks in your mutual fund, the others will help buffer the loss and may even help make up for it. If your individual stock goes down the tubes, you've got no safety net, and a lot less money.

This definitely aided my million-dollars-by-thirty goal. But it wasn't something I had planned on. It's important to understand that in markets of any kind, extreme swings like this can occur. Up and down. The stock market in the 1990s had record days all because of the unforeseen dot-com boom. Likewise, it had a big downfall after the dot-com bubble burst. It wasn't unheard of that those in a good stock position could see their money double overnight. However, many of these same people saw the reverse effect as the market went back down just as fast. Now the real-estate market was having the same sort of success. And I benefited handsomely, just because I accidentally happened to be involved in the hot market at the time.

ALAN COREY 101

You can't predict markets. So-called experts try all the time, and no one is 100 percent correct. The best strategy is investing heavily and often in many different markets. That way, if one market takes off, you are in a position to benefit. The thing to remember is that all of this came about because I had invested heavily and often in both the stock market and the real-estate market. The stock market could have seen another huge boom, and I would have benefited from my 401(k), Roth IRA, and mutual fund investments. On the other hand, my money was evenly distributed, so if one market had an extreme downfall, I wouldn't have lost every single penny I had. Having an investment portfolio of different markets meant that I had different opportunities to take advantage of these freak occurrences. Plus, with the resurgence of all the investing, the economy improved, increasing the value of my stocks.

Basically, if I hadn't created this balanced situation for myself, then I never would have been able to be "lucky." Putting all your eggs in one basket, or one market, has the potential to make you extremely lucky or extremely unlucky. I was fine just being lucky.

AGE TWENTY-EIGHT

Checking account: $8,000

Savings account: $172,000

Second, hidden savings account: $?

401(k): $35,250

Mutual fund: $17,750

Roth IRA: $15,800

Equity on house: $587,000 ($985,000 new estimated value – $398,000 mortgage)

Equity on bar and restaurant: $60,000

Total net worth: $895,800

Chapter 24
Declaration of Independence

I'M *rich! I'm finally rich. I have reached all my subgoals along the way to being a millionaire by thirty and have just a little bit more to go. It's just a waiting game now. If I just hold on to my job for another year or so, I'll make it. If the stock market or real-estate market goes up, I'll make it in even less than six months. I can't believe it! I'm almost there!*

At the age of twenty-eight, I was getting really close to my goal, and I was way ahead of schedule. I continued investing in all my stocks and keeping an eye on the still-rising real-estate market in New York City. For the first time in five years, I felt like I could cut back on my extreme saving and enjoy life a little bit. I went out more, because for once, I could be the person buying drinks at the bar. (Although this was done only on special occasions, as I was still a cheapskate at heart.) I went on several vacations around the world, crossing off items on my life's *other* to-do list. This was costing me a lot on my twelve-more-months-on-the-day-job-till-I'm-a-millionaire plan, but I needed to take a break and enjoy life a bit.

If I hadn't benefited from the unique and beneficial condition of the real-estate market, I still would have had another two years to add around $250,000 to my net worth to be a millionaire by thirty. I would have put those vacations on hold. As it turned out, I had gained $187,000 in an unforeseen occurrence and now had a little over $100,000 to go. I had no expenses, so my salary of around $55,000 was being invested in its entirety, and I was still making money on the rental units in my house. Honestly, I'm not sure what I would have done over the next two years if the real estate market didn't take off like it did. Maybe I would have done another house flip, maybe more home renovations, or maybe another bar purchase. I figured it would have taken only one more solid investment to reach my goal of being a millionaire by the age of thirty, and I would have made it even without the "luckiness" factor of the soaring real-estate market. It helped me get closer, but I wasn't there just yet.

All this didn't stop me from closely monitoring my bank account. I was so close, I obviously didn't want to lose what I had accomplished. My millionaire status was within reach at the age of twenty-eight. I had only a little bit more to go, and it was time to check my hidden bank account to see exactly just how much I still needed.

After heading crosstown, I found out that I had $29,200 in my hidden bank account! That was a great present to myself; a reward for living below my means for the last few years. The best reward, though: I had only $20,000 more to make this year (after investing my entire $55,000 day-job salary) to be a millionaire by thirty! I knew I could get it done this year; just investing the huge chunk of money in my savings account into a mutual fund with a better rate of return would do wonders. I felt that with patience and a few minor changes, I could get this millionaire goal done sooner rather than later. Given all I had accomplished, all the knowledge I had gathered, and all the advice I could give, I felt I should take the lessons I learned along the way and put them to good use. Surely someone could benefit from my experiences. I still wasn't a financial expert, still had no defined skills, yet I was really close to achieving a huge financial milestone in a short amount of time. I thought a personal finance book would really help other people, as I was just a regular mumbling Joe with no previous knowledge of investing, just a mission to get rich. I didn't see why anyone else couldn't follow in my steps and accomplish the same. I thought getting a book published could also be my new subgoal if I did end up a bit short on my millionaire status.

A few years before, I had created a personal Web site wonderfully named alancorey.com. (I knew better than to call it bigal.com.) My site was my personal marketing tool for whatever project I was working on at the time. It consisted mainly of a few photos, some of my press clippings, contact information, and a short bio. It was rarely updated and, thus, rarely visited. I updated the last line in my short biography to say, "Alan is currently at work on a book about investing in your twenties." Which was merely one more motivational tool to get me working on my latest project. By writing it down, I had created a visual reminder of my goal, and I saw it staring back at me every time I went to my Web site.

A few friends asked me about it, and I told them of my idea. I hadn't actually written anything down yet, but I was bouncing around the concept in my head and trying to figure out how to get a book deal. Here I was, twenty-eight, crazy (or naïve) enough to set a new large, looming subgoal of getting published just in case the right opportunity came along. I knew a book deal was a long shot, but with the life experiences I had built over the years—from doing everything from living in the projects to learning how to be a landlord on the fly—I felt like I could accomplish anything. I would regret not trying, that's for sure. I just wanted to challenge myself and see if I could do it.

I figured I had a unique hook, similar to the creative approaches I had used to getting on reality TV. I was so close to being a millionaire before thirty, and I did it without a huge income. If I could do it, anyone could. Who wouldn't want to read about that? My story was unique but applicable to others. So I resorted to doing what I always do. I bought several books on the subject of getting published. And as I started my research of getting a book deal, I felt just like I had when I first started my journey into finance: delusional optimism.

As I was at home reading my "how to write a book" books, an editor from a major publishing house in New York was online reading about how Barbara Corcoran bought my building in Brooklyn. Curbed, a major New York real-estate blog, had written about it and had a link to my Web site, specifically to my bio page.

The big-time editor saw in my bio that I was "currently at work on a book about investing in your twenties." And as chance would have it (or, more likely, through the amazing power of the press), she sent me an e-mail to see if I was looking for a publisher. She liked my story and saw a market for it. I told her of course I was, without revealing that I hadn't actually put anything on paper yet. She told me to send her my book proposal, and she'd see what she could do. I was jumping up and down! I couldn't stop thinking this might be the final piece to my puzzle. But I didn't have a book proposal. I barely knew what one was. I wrote one as fast as I could, stealing a layout from the example in one of my books. I had no real outline or overall concept; it was really just words on paper. I just wanted to get something in her hands before she forgot about me. A month later, I sent her my thirty-page proposal, and I admit it was a mess. I was definitely out of my league in knowing how to write a book based on just reading a few books about it.

She, of course, hated it, and told me that I needed to work with a literary agent to help me refine it and make it presentable. I was happy with that and thankful that she didn't just say, "Get lost." She introduced me to an agent she thought highly of, and we had some meetings over the phone. He gave me some pointers and some basic guidelines. It took me another three months to rewrite the proposal, and once I was finished, I sent it to him. If this went perfectly, he would fall in love with my proposal, sell it quickly, and I'd be a millionaire by twenty-eight.

Well, he hated it as well. (Well, maybe not hated it, but he said it definitely was not ready for prime time and needed work.) But he didn't say "Get lost" either. Instead he referred me to a freelance editor he thought highly of to help me write a new proposal. I was frustrated but still holding on to hope. Mainly, I saw that I was working my way *down* the totem pole. I started with a major publishing house, was pushed down to an agent, and then was pushed down to a freelance editor. I had to find a way to work myself back up to the top.

Another four months passed as I worked with the editor on getting a decent proposal put together. I really liked her, and from my previous experience with working with people, I knew a great partner when I saw one. She was worth every penny. By the time I finished working with her, I had another version of my book proposal to try to pitch. I brought it back to the agent, and he liked it. *Relief.* All that was left now was to give it back to the editor from the publishing house who had originally contacted me, to see if *she* liked it. I was getting excited. My finish line was in sight.

When I went to send it to her, I encountered another obstacle: The editor no longer worked there! In the year that had passed, she had switched jobs. I had lost my main contact to the publishing world. Luckily she was right, and the agent she had referred me to was top notch. He believed in the project and said he'd pitch it to other publishing houses. He told me it would take probably about three months before I heard anything, and not to get my hopes up. Not very encouraging, but it was all I had. I crossed my fingers.

Thankfully, I eventually got some good news. A publishing house even bigger than the one that had originally contacted me wanted to publish it. Despite my new, less-frugal lifestyle, the book advance it offered was indeed enough to push me over the threshold to millionaire status. I had accomplished two goals at the same time: I got a book deal and became a millionaire before thirty on the same day! Even more rewarding, I had done it a month shy of my twenty-ninth birthday.

Instantly, I quit the day job. (Yes, I gave two weeks' notice. I may be a millionaire, but I'm still not an asshole.) I then threw an awesome "retirement" party at my bar to celebrate both my book deal and leaving my day job. Retirement is just telling the world that if I want to be bored, it's now on my terms! And then, probably like most people do, I began my retirement nursing a multiday hangover. I wouldn't have wanted it any other way.

Now at twenty-nine, I am in a position to no longer have another boss again. I am financially comfortable, with multiple income sources, and I'm free to do as I please. My penny-pinching ways may have caused me to miss out on many parties and bar-hopping experiences and unnecessary shopping trips when I first moved to New York. But the payoff is that now I can go out any time of day and night and not have to work forty hours a week. It's not that bad to have a day job—as you know, I had one for six years. But now I don't miss any more fun events, because I'm a millionaire before thirty! On the other hand, I still live in a windowless office, still have the same old TV, still have no exceptional talents, and am still a bit scared of the opposite sex. Money doesn't change everything. Evil genius, rock star, comedian—none of that worked out for me. But being a millionaire before thirty did. Now it's your turn!

ALAN COREY 101

If I can do it, you can do it. Focus on your goal, and once you reach it, it will all be worth it. There are several ways to be a millionaire. This was my way. I couldn't completely control my income, but I made sure to control my outcome. I did it in the most expensive city in America; you can do it in your city too. Take the points that work for you, educate yourself on what you don't understand, and put a plan into action. There's a million dollars waiting for you at the end. Enjoy it! (And when you get there, send me a thank-you card. The ones that come with money.)

For the record, the first thing I bought with my book advance was a brand-new iPod. I still believe it was worth the wait. Now I just need to figure out how to put music on the damn thing.

AGE TWENTY-NINE

Checking account: $40,000

Savings account: $182,750

Second, hidden savings account: $29,200

401(k): $42,700

Mutual fund: $23,000

Roth IRA: $20,350

Equity on house: $587,000

Equity on bar and restaurant: $75,000

Total net worth: $1 million!

Acnowlegements

I would like to acknowledge that I misspelled *acknowledg-ments.* (I pay my editor by the page.)

I would like to send one thousand thank-yous to everyone who believed in this book from day one. It would not have been possible without the encouragement of my agent, Barret "Barry" Neville, the editing of Martha "Mimi" O'Connor, and the foresight of Michelle "Foresight Eyes" Howry.

Many thanks also to Christina Duffy at Random House. If you didn't believe in this book, I would not have been able to tell the world I got Miss Universe's phone number.

My extended gratitude goes to Sadia Perveen, Roy "Buddy" Kite, and Roger Hailes for their input on the book. You helped make this happen.

I would like it to be known that I would not have been able to be a millionaire by thirty without the help of many people. It took a team:

Much appreciation to my family for supporting me in everything I do (well, 95 percent of everything I do). Mom and Dad, thanks for being great teachers. Al Hawkins, thanks for marrying Jill. Jill, thanks for marrying Al.

I would like to thank the entire Leonard family for their generosity, support, and love over the last eight years. You guys make great friends and partners. Thank you so much for being so great. Katie, your family is a bottomless soup of pleasure. (That's a good thing.)

A big part of my success belongs to the Farrells. Thanks for being excellent neighbors and being a big part of my New York life. I couldn't have done it without you.

Handshakes and smiles to the staff of Pioneer Bar-B-Q; although the bar has been sold and changed, your hard work was much appreciated. High fives to Matt Hake and Phil Jean; you two guys are the only moneylenders I've ever seen wearing a girl's bathing suit. Financial shout-out to Jeff Palmiotti; thanks for buying into all my schemes. Many praises to Andrew Wright for booking "The Seagulls" a televised gig. Paddy Owls, thanks for the rivalry. To my ex-girlfriends, you are queens for putting up with all my money neuroses. I know it wasn't easy. To my accountant, Joel Rosenberg, and real-estate attorney, Michael Neary, thanks for all the boring yet wonderful business advice. Head nods to Chris Kula and Charlie Todd for their comedic and bargain-friendly brains over the years. Hugs and kisses to the DPG, a marvelously loyal group of hooligans.

And, lastly, cheers to my basketball coaches, Joe Prince and Dave Pittman. You guys didn't help me make any money, but you helped me perfect an unstoppable baseline drive. That, as they say, is priceless.

Glossary

All cash deal Real-estate slang meaning that the buyer is not getting a mortgage to purchase the property but will be paying for the property in full at the closing (although this is usually done with a certified check rather than a van full of cash). (See page 179)

Brokerage account Places that will help you invest online include E*Trade Financial and Charles Schwab & Co. A brokerage account is one that allows you to buy stocks, bonds, mutual funds, and other investments by telling an accredited broker what you want. Most of the transactions are done online and can be accomplished without having to talk to anyone. (You can choose to talk to someone if you prefer.) (See page 55)

Capital gains tax Tax on a sale of an asset that has increased in value during your ownership. Stocks, real estate, bonds, and precious metals have different tax rules, but real estate is very favorable taxwise to investors. (See page 154)

Closing The official completion of a real-estate transaction (the day all the papers are signed). (See page 71)

Comparables The most common way to determine a property's value is to compare the prices of similar properties nearby that have recently sold. Check out Trulia.com to access recent sale prices in your neighborhood. (See page 111)

Compound interest Interest paid on the principal plus the already accumulated interest. Each year, you are compounding a higher amount as interest accumulates. The more often something is compounded, the larger your principal, or your money invested increases. This is why compound interest is so advantageous to young investors. (See page 40)

Contractors and handymen To locate contractors and handymen, it is always best to go with a reference. Talk to friends, family, and neighbors in the area to see who they have used and liked. Ask how much the person charged, if he showed up on time, and, obviously, if he did a good job. Ask the contractors for their own references, go see examples of their work, and ask a lot of questions. A bad contractor or handyman will make things miserable for you. (See page 109)

Credit score A credit score is a three-digit ranking based on your credit history that helps lenders determine your credit worthiness, meaning how good of a borrower you will be. The higher your credit score, the better interest rates you will get on loans. Your credit score can range from 300 to 900, but anything over 700 is considered excellent. (See page 32)

Dollar cost averaging This is a strategy of investing regularly regardless of market conditions. You invest the same amount in the stock or mutual fund on a regular basis, not worrying if the price is high or low. Over the long term, you're averaging out and spending the actual cost of the investment. This makes trying to time the market unnecessary. (See page 60)

Down payment Amount you pay at the closing to secure a real-estate purchase. The remainder is paid with a mortgage. Down payments are not always necessary, but it's typical to pay a down payment of 10 percent to 20 percent of the purchase price. Think of it this way: the purchase price − mortgage amount = down payment ($100,000 PP − $90,000 MA = $10,000 DP). (See page 66)

Emergency fund Saving up three months' worth of living expenses that is entirely hands-off except in case of emergency (illness, losing a job, death of car, and so on). A wise—and crucial—financial strategy. (See page 123)

Equity The value of a piece of property minus the money you owe on it. (See page 71)

Exclusive agreement An agreement to list your property with only one real-estate company for a defined period of time. The benefits include a more focused marketing of the building, as it is theirs only for a limited time, plus a negotiable or reduced broker commission. (See page 177)

Flipping property Real-estate slang for an investment strategy of buying a house in poor condition, renovating it quickly, and reselling it. This "flip" of the property can return great profits but is considered a risky investment for beginners. (See page 180)

Foreclosure When a bank repossesses a property because of missed mortgage payments. Banks then sell the property to get their money back. (See page 168)

For sale by owner Selling property without the use of a real-estate agent. This saves owners from paying a commission for selling their property. However, owners usually are not real-estate experts, and this can lead to less exposure of their property, underpriced properties, and having to negotiate directly with the buyer rather than through the agent. (See page 161)

401(k) A 401(k) is an employer-sponsored retirement plan. Money is taken from your paycheck before it is taxed (which may put you into a lower tax bracket) and invested in a retirement fund for you (usually in a form of mutual funds). Many times companies will match your 401(k) contribution. For instance, if you elect to automatically invest 5 percent of your paycheck in your 401(k), your company will match that 5 percent, essentially doubling your investment. I recommend investing in 401(k)s as soon as possible and contributing the maximum amount possible. These funds can be transferred from job to job or from a job fund to personal 401(k) accounts with brokerage firms (Charles Schwab & Co., E*Trade Financial, and so on). It's one of the smartest, easiest, and most cost-effective ways to build a nest egg. (See page 26)

Good faith estimate You will receive a GFE within three days of applying for a mortgage. This will be a "good faith" outline of all the up-front expenses that you will incur by accepting this loan. It's best to consider this the lowest amount you will have to spend at the closing. Remember, although the estimates are in good faith, they aren't completely accurate, sometimes reflecting a much lower expense than you will actually incur. (See page 71)

Gut renovation Stripping down a property to its framing, and replacing everything from floors, to walls, to ceilings. (See page 110)

Home equity A home equity loan or line of credit allows homeowners to borrow money using their property's equity as collateral. (See page 168)

Interest Think of interest as the "rental fee" you owe for borrowed money. If you charge $1,000 on your credit card, that borrowed money is called the *principal*. You will be charged a rental fee based on a percentage of the principal in order to borrow that money. That percentage (and your rental fee) is called *interest*. For example, if your credit card charges $2 a day interest for borrowing $1,000 in principal, the math would be $2 a day per $1,000 principal = .2 percent a day interest. (See page 25)

Interest rates Interest rates change for a variety of reasons, but it's mainly based on the strength of the economy. If the economy is doing poorly, interest rates are lowered to help encourage investments. If the economy is gaining ground, the rates are raised to keep a nice balance and to control inflation. (See page 118)

Liquid An asset that can easily be turned into cash. Stocks can be sold quickly; therefore they are considered a very liquid investment. Real estate takes time to sell, so it is not considered very liquid. (See page 66)

Lowball offer A negotiation strategy where you purposely put in an offer for less than what you think the property is worth. (See page 70)

Mortgage A loan for the purpose of buying real estate. There are many different kinds of mortgages, such as a thirty-year fixed and a five-year ARM, or adjustable rate mortgage. A thirty-year fixed mortgage means you have thirty years to pay it off at a fixed interest rate, and your monthly payment doesn't change for the life of the loan. A five-year ARM means the interest rate is fixed for five years; it will adjust itself to the current interest rate thereafter. (See page 66)

Mortgage broker Recommendations are the best way to go when locating a good mortgage broker. Brokers don't get paid unless they find you a loan you agree on. For instance, he might find you a loan at 6 percent interest (pretty good), but he works on commission, so he'll give it to you at 6.5 percent interest (still pretty good). These added percentage points the broker gives you are sometimes negotiable. It doesn't hurt to try. Always ask up front if there are any other hidden fees. If you have a decent credit score, there shouldn't be. And lastly, you can avoid all commission fees on a loan by working with a bank directly rather than through a broker. The only drawback is that it usually takes more time, and therefore more hassle, dealing with banks than with brokers. (See page 112)

Multifamily home Real-estate property that has more than one unit. This can be anything from a two-family town-house to a twenty-plus-unit apartment complex. (See page 114)

Mutual fund Mutual funds are investment funds in which investors pool money together and invest based on a decision of a fund manager. The manager buys various forms of stocks and securities to try to get the best return possible for all the investors. Mutual funds often have themes, such as index mutual funds, which invest only in the S&P (Standard & Poor's) 500 index (the five hundred biggest stock companies), and property index funds, which invest in real estate. Many have a minimum investment amount, but you can find some that don't. Investing in no-load and low-fee mutual funds is crucial, as you don't want to be paying commission and sales charges that will wipe out any profit you may have gained. (See page 26)

Open house A way to sell real estate by opening up the house to all visitors at a scheduled time for a walk-through of the property. A real-estate agent usually hosts the tour, and the homeowners are usually absent. (See page 68)

Partnership A written business contract through which all partners agree to share profits and expenses of the business. I would recommend having the partnership agreement overseen by a lawyer or an accountant who can file it with the state. This usually can be done for less than $300. (See page 154)

Portfolio A collection of all your investments. Having diversification and investing in different areas within your portfolio will reduce risk (in other words, not having all your eggs in one basket). (See page 66)

Positive cash flow A situation in which income is greater than expenses. Having a credit card that rewards you with cash back, as long as you pay off the balance in full each month, creates a positive cash flow situation. (See page 27)

Press release A press release is a news bulletin sent via fax or e-mail to media outlets informing them of a potential story. Anyone is free to submit a press release. (See page 145)

Real-estate agent's fee An agreed-upon commission paid to the real-estate agent for his/her role in the transaction of real estate. Usually it's a percentage of the sales price (roughly 2 percent to 6 percent), and negotiable. You pay only if the transaction is completed. (See page 179)

Refinance Replacing your old mortgage with a new mortgage, usually one with more favorable rates. Usually done when interest rates are lowered or the value of your property has gone up drastically. Refinancing allows you to lower monthly payments or cash out some equity. (See page 191)

Roth IRA A Roth IRA is an Individual Retirement Account that is usually invested in stocks. Roths are different than other IRAs in that all earnings made from your contribution are tax free. Starting in 2008, you can contribute up to $5,000 a year to your Roth IRA account, and all the money you earn is yours; no tax will have to be paid on it. An advantage of a Roth IRA is that there are no age limits for when you can cash out your money. A disadvantage is that you cannot contribute to a Roth IRA if you make over $95,000 a year. (See page 26)

Rule of 72 This rule will help you figure out how long it will take to double your money. Just divide 72 by the growth rate. For instance, if you invested $250 once at 9 percent, it would take eight years for your investment to be worth double that ($500), as $72 \div 9\% = 8$ years. (See page 51)

Savings Bond Savings bonds are obligations owed to you by the U.S. government. The government issues bonds to raise money in the present by promising to pay you back more in the future. The way it does that is to sell a bond at discount (for instance, half of face value). After a specified period of time (say eight to ten years), the bond will mature to be worth the value it was issued for. (See page 33)

Socially responsible investing Not all corporations are evil. You can also choose to invest your money with only socially responsible and environmentally friendly companies. Certain brokerage houses, like Calvert, specialize in socially responsible mutual funds to help you become a socially responsible investor. You create your standards, and then it invests your money only in these "good" companies. (See page 56)

Solid buyer Real-estate slang meaning that the buyer is of solid financial background and thus will not have trouble being approved for a mortgage, which would kill a real-estate transaction. (See page 177)

Timing the market Timing the market is the bad-idea strategy used by many beginners trying to predict when the market is about to go up and when the market is going to go down, and then selling/buying stocks based on that hunch. (See page 49)

Traditional IRA Similar to a Roth, it's another form of an Individual Retirement Account. However, unlike the Roth, traditional IRAs are subject to income taxes based on the money they have made. It also differs in that your contributions are tax deductible. (See page 26)

Transitional neighborhoods Up-and-coming neighborhoods. You can usually tell if a neighborhood is improving by noticing if any construction projects are happening on the block. (If neighbors are investing money in fixing up their property, that's a good sign.) Also, commercial places nearby say a lot. If artsy new restaurants are opening up, or a retail store that's a big step up from a 99-cent store, that usually means the neighborhood is changing too. Restaurant owners and boutique store owners are by definition entrepreneurs, and successful ones see things well in advance. So feel free to ride their coattails and follow them into a new neighborhood, as they would appreciate new residents moving in as well. Now, realize that neighborhoods don't change overnight; it's a slow multiyear process. But it can do wonders for your investments if you just have the patience for a transitional neighborhood to turn around. (See page 68)

ALAN COREY is a New York City–based entrepreneur, speaker, writer, and bargain hunter. A bit of a fame whore, he has appeared on five reality TV shows and one game show to date and is still looking for more.

Visit his Web site at www.alancorey.com.